WALKI

HOWGILL FELLS

HILLSIDE GUIDES - ACROSS THE NORTH

The Uplands of Britain
- **THE HIGH PEAKS OF ENGLAND & WALES**
- **YORKSHIRE DALES, MOORS & FELLS**

Long Distance Walks
- **COAST TO COAST WALK**
- **DALES WAY**
- **CLEVELAND WAY**
- **CUMBRIA WAY**
- **WESTMORLAND WAY**
- **FURNESS WAY**
- **BRONTE WAY**
- **PENDLE WAY**
- **NIDDERDALE WAY**
- **LADY ANNE'S WAY**
- **TRANS-PENNINE WAY**
- **CALDERDALE WAY**

Hillwalking - Lake District
- **LAKELAND FELLS - SOUTH**
- **LAKELAND FELLS - EAST**
- **LAKELAND FELLS - NORTH**
- **LAKELAND FELLS - WEST**

Circular Walks - Peak District
- **NORTHERN PEAK**
- **EASTERN PEAK**
- **CENTRAL PEAK**
- **SOUTHERN PEAK**
- **WESTERN PEAK**

Circular Walks - Yorkshire Dales
- **HOWGILL FELLS**
- **THREE PEAKS**
- **MALHAMDALE**
- **WHARFEDALE**
- **NIDDERDALE**
- **WENSLEYDALE**
- **SWALEDALE**

Circular Walks - North York Moors
- **WESTERN MOORS**
- **SOUTHERN MOORS**

Circular Walks - South Pennines
- **BRONTE COUNTRY**
- **CALDERDALE**
- **SOUTHERN PENNINES**
- **ILKLEY MOOR**
- **HARROGATE & WHARFE VALLEY**

Circular Walks - Lancashire
- **BOWLAND**
- **PENDLE & THE RIBBLE**
- **WEST PENNINE MOORS**

Circular Walks - North Pennines
- **TEESDALE**
- **EDEN VALLEY**
- **ALSTON & ALLENDALE**

City Theme Walks
- **YORK WALKS**

WayMaster Guides - Short Scenic Walks
- **WHARFEDALE**
- **AMBLESIDE & LANGDALE**

- **AIRE VALLEY BIKING GUIDE**
- **CALDERDALE BIKING GUIDE**
- **WHARFEDALE BIKING GUIDE**

WayMaster Visitor Guides • **YORKSHIRE DALES**

Send for a detailed current catalogue and pricelist,
and also visit *www.hillsidepublications.co.uk*

HOWGILL FELLS

Paul Hannon

HILLSIDE

HILLSIDE
PUBLICATIONS
12 Broadlands
Shann Park
Keighley
West Yorkshire
BD20 6HX

First published 1992
Extended 1997
4th impression 2006

ISBN 1 870141 49 0
ISBN (from 2007) 978-1-870141-49-9

Whilst the author has walked and researched all the routes for the purposes of this guide, no responsibility can be accepted for any unforeseen circumstances encountered while following them. The publisher would, however, greatly appreciate any information regarding material changes, and any problems encountered.

Cover illustration:
The Howgills from the south-west
Back cover: The Calf from under Fell Head;
Carlingill; Winter at Cautley Spout
(Paul Hannon/Hillslides Picture Library)

Page 1: Black Force, Carlingill
Page 3: Harter Fell from Black Moss, Uldale

Printed in Great Britain by
Carnmor Print
95-97 London Road
Preston
Lancashire
PR1 4BA

CONTENTS

INTRODUCTION

The Howgill Fells are a compact, well defined upland range, situated in the north-west corner of the Yorkshire Dales, yet wholly within Cumbria. Triangular in shape, the group is moated by the Lune on two sides and the Rawthey on the other. Across these rivers is further unsung country that merits more than a passing glance, and so the scope of this guide extends to include the likes of Uldale, Garsdale, Borrowdale, Bretherdale and the Frostrow Fells. The wooded riverbanks and colourful foothills are integral parts of the area, adding diversity of scenery to the Howgills' special grandeur.

The hub of this otherwise sparsely populated district is the market town of Sedbergh, while the supporting villages of Ravenstonedale and Tebay tidily occupy the other two corners of the Howgills patch. A little further afield is the market town of Kirkby Stephen, while the nearest large town is Kendal. The fells are named from a settlement scattered along the western base - rather than the obvious choice of Sedbergh - and even this only found its way onto maps in quite recent times. This alone may have helped keep the hills relatively undisturbed: certainly more people gasp at their splendour from 70mph on the motorway than ever set foot on their inviting slopes.

The Howgill Fells rise to more than 2000ft (610m), and provide five independent mountains. Additionally there are several lesser 2000ft tops and a whole range of lower summits along the radiating ridges and outer fringes. The terrain of the Howgill Fells encourages long strides over its grassy ridges, a lack of internal walls instilling a sense of freedom not sensed elsewhere in the Dales. Walkers have always enjoyed de facto access to this open country, virtually all of which now falls within Open Access land. Of course our responsibilities remain: dogs should be kept under firm control (preferably on a lead) in this sheep farming landscape, while the privacy of the small, intimate settlements around the base of the hills should be respected.

Rarely in evidence is the underlying slate, though when revealed it is done in some style, at the remarkable ravines of Cautley and Carlingill. This walkers' paradise is a no-man's-land where Dales and Lakes meet, the characteristics of both being present with neither dominating. This identity crisis is fuelled by the fact that only half of the main group falls within the National Park, for the northern dales and ridges of old Westmorland are accorded no such protection.

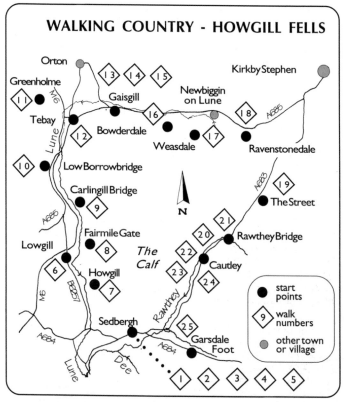

WALKING COUNTRY - HOWGILL FELLS

THE COUNTRY CODE
- Respect the life and work of the countryside
- Protect wildlife, plants and trees
- Keep to public paths across farmland
- Safeguard water supplies
- Go carefully on country roads
- Keep dogs under control
- Guard against all risks of fire
- Fasten all gates
- Leave no litter - take it with you
- Make no unnecessary noise
- Leave livestock, crops and machinery alone
- Use gates and stiles to cross fences, hedges and walls

7

The increasing popularity of the area is apparent to those who knew it just a few years ago. Don't be misled by the fact that here are fells rising to over 2000ft. This is not the Lake District, and other than in winter it creates unnecessary damage to the hill paths to tramp round in thumping great boots: gentle, lightweight footwear is perfectly adequate for most folk. Only at Cautley and Carlingill is there anything like rough country.

The one long distance walk likely to be encountered is the popular Dales Way. This enters the area in Dentdale, passing Sedbergh and tracing the Lune before heading off for the Lakes at Lowgill. In spite of its isolation the area is ringed by main roads, and is made further accessible by the Settle-Carlisle Railway, a most practical as well as a scenically magnificent line.

Sedbergh

Sedbergh is a smashing little town, and the largest community in the Yorkshire Dales National Park. Its isolation has, however, helped it avoid the excesses of commercialism. Ceded to Cumbria in 1974, Sedbergh - omit the 'gh' in pronunciation - was previously in the north-western extremity of the West Riding of Yorkshire, incredibly over 100 miles distant from its West Riding colleague Sheffield. Two simple facts illustrating size is very much a relative thing.

This tiny market town boasts an unparalleled position on the lower slopes of its 'own' mountains the Howgill Fells, and the outlook on three sides is, in fact, of fells. This is the edge of the Dales, and to the west of the town runs the river Lune. In the neighbourhood of Sedbergh three lively rivers end their journeys, as the Dee, Clough and Rawthey join forces to swell the waters of the Lune.

Aside from the imposing Howgill Fells, Sedbergh itself is dominated by its public school. This famous establishment, which was founded in the early 16th century, includes Adam Sedgwick the geologist and Will Carling, record-breaking England rugby captain among its old boys. The oldest remaining part dates from 1716 and is now the library. Most other features of interest will be found on or near the lengthy main street, including a lovely parish church in an equally attractive wooded surround. Dedicated to St. Andrew it has a 15th century tower, with other parts dating back to Norman times as well as many other periods in between. Overlooking the eastern end of town is the distinctive motte and bailey site of Castlehaw.

Getting around

The area is ideally placed for access from the M6 motorway (junctions 37 or 38), south-eastern Lakeland and the western and northern quarters of the Yorkshire Dales. The Settle-Carlisle Railway offers approaches via Dent, Garsdale and Kirkby Stephen stations. Without doubt Sedbergh is the finest base, though Kirkby Stephen, Tebay and the villages in between are also well placed for many walks. Public transport within the area is sparse, but a brief comment on availability, where applicable, is given at the start of each walk.

Using the guide

Each walk is self-contained, essential information being followed by a concise route description and a simple map. Dovetailed between this are useful notes of features along the way, and interspersed are illustrations which both capture the flavour of the walks and depict many of the items of interest. In order to make the directions easier to follow, essential route description has been highlighted in bold type, while items in lighter type refer to historical asides and things to look out for: in this format you can find your way more easily while still locating features of interest at the relevant point in the text. Please remember that over time details can change and paths can be opened, closed or diverted: always follow legitimate instructions that over-ride those in the guide.

Maps

The simple sketch maps identify the location of the routes rather than the fine detail, and whilst the route description should be sufficient to guide you around, an Ordnance Survey map is recommended. The route can easily be plotted on the relevant OS map. To gain the most from a walk, the remarkable detail of the 1:25,000 scale maps cannot be matched. They also serve to vary walks as desired, giving an improved picture of one's surroundings and the availability of linking paths. The area is covered by three Explorer maps, and these sheets serve the following walk numbers:

- Explorer OL2 - *Yorkshire Dales South/West* (4,5,25)
- Explorer OL7 - *English Lakes South East* (10,11)
- Explorer OL19 - *Howgill Fells/Upper Eden Valley* (1-10,12-25)

Ideal for general planning are the Landranger maps (1:50,000 scale), and the following sheets cover the area: 97 Kendal to Morecambe; 91 Appleby-in-Westmorland; 98 Wensleydale & Upper Wharfedale.

Also extremely useful is the *HOWGILL FELLS* map at a scale of 1:25,000 produced by Harvey Maps.

THE CALF

START *Sedbergh*   *Grid ref. SD 658921*

DISTANCE *7¾ miles/12½km*

ORDNANCE SURVEY MAPS
1:50,000
Landranger 97 - Kendal to Morecambe
Landranger 98 - Wensleydale & Upper Wharfedale
1:25,000
Explorer OL19 - Howgill Fells/Upper Eden Valley

ACCESS *Start from the town centre. There are two central car parks. Sedbergh has infrequent bus links with Kendal, Kirkby Stephen and Dent.*

A classic ascent, and no better walk exists for the first-time visitor.

S Leave the main street by Joss Lane rising past the main car park. It swings up to the right: 'to the fell' signs ease the way out of town. From the lane's demise at a gate a farm road to Hill takes over, while our way slants to the top corner of a field. A path climbs with Settlebeck Gill to gain the open fell at a quaint old kissing-gate. Already there is a smashing prospect over the town and its attendant dales and hills.

Take the green path slanting up behind a seat, quickly doubling back to run high above the gill. Slowly deflected away from it by a tiny side-stream, the path reaches a broad upland basin. Here take the path bearing right, back to the edge of the gill, and continue upstream. Remain with the gill to rise to the main Howgills pathway. This is a great moment, with your impending path climbing to Arant Haw and beyond, and the Lune Valley backed by a Lakeland skyline. Over to the right is the prominent cairn on Crook.

Stride on in style towards Arant Haw on this broad path. Scaling its similarly broad south ridge, the path veers right across a shoulder of the fell. Ahead now, the bolder top of Calders awaits across the depression of Rowantree Grains. **Descending to the saddle a steeper pull leads by a fence to suddenly gain the cairn on Calders.** The fence turns away just short of the top. At 2211ft/674m this summit is a fine vantage point, resting on the edge of a more pronounced drop than the principal summit of the group. Also, it is only now that the Calf finally reveals itself, the trig. point being just 15 minutes away.

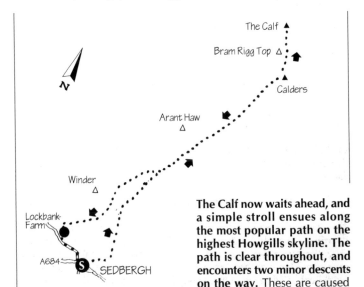

The Calf now waits ahead, and a simple stroll ensues along the most popular path on the highest Howgills skyline. The path is clear throughout, and encounters two minor descents on the way. These are caused by the intervening minor top of Bram Rigg Top. At 2204ft/672m the highest point is 150 yards to the left, marked by a tiny cairn. **The final pull is a very short one to the OS column (S5676) marking the summit of the Calf at 2218ft/676m.**

Although this highest point on the Howgills ensures the widest views, the Calf's plateau restricts interesting foregrounds to the Lune Valley, westwards. The rest of the panorama is limited to more distant scenes, featuring the Cross Fell group to the north and the widely spread hills of the Dales to east and south. On a clear day, however, the serrated Lakeland skyline to the west will claim most attention.

The summit of The Calf, looking west to Fell Head

The return route offers scope for variation by adding the intervening tops of Arant Haw and Winder. If not doing so, it is nevertheless worth a lower variation, by omitting Settlebeck Gill and remaining on the main path along the eastern flank of Winder. This then slants across its southern face high above the town to double back down to the rear of Lockbank Farm. From the gate drop down a short green way into the yard, emerging via the farm drive (a permissive path) onto Howgill Lane, turning left to finish.

St Andrew's church, Sedbergh

2

DOWBIGGIN

START Sedbergh   Grid ref. SD 658921

DISTANCE 6½ miles/10½km

ORDNANCE SURVEY MAPS
1:50,000
Landranger 98 - Wensleydale & Upper Wharfedale
1:25,000
Explorer OL19 - Howgill Fells/Upper Eden Valley

ACCESS There are two car parks in the centre of Sedbergh, though the lay-by at New Bridge is actually most handily placed. Infrequent bus links with Kendal, Kirkby Stephen and Dent.

A fascinating perambulation by two rivers and two gills. The walk's intimate river scenery is equalled by extensive views from the base of the fell, with the Howgills majestic in their entirety from Winder to Wandale Hill.

⑤ From the main street head east to branch right on the Hawes road at the edge of town. Soon after crossing New Bridge the road narrows, and care is needed. On the left you pass the former pinfold (once used for collecting stray farm animals) by the entrance to a caravan site. **The first junction on the left brings relief as a rough lane runs down to Garsdale Bridge.** The mill here is very large for the locality, and is still put to some use. This is a lovely spot, with the presence of the Dent Fault ensuring superior river scenery.

Cross the bridge and take a stile to shadow the Clough upstream. Above a wooded bank the path descends to the river, and now adheres to its winding course until just past a footbridge. Here you are deflected up by another wooded bank. This time there is no return to the riverbank, for the sketchy path that has materialised

maintains its rise over the pastures, on a generally obvious line to a stile before a marshy enclosure. Bearing left here, a clearer track forms and skirts round to the left. At the end it swings left to a gate, and here go right to the next gate where a short-lived stony, enclosed way climbs to Dowbiggin Lane.

Turn right along its narrow course, and keep straight on along the short drive to Dovecote Gill. Passing between the farm buildings, take a gate on the right to drop to the wooded environs of the gill itself. Notices advise the wooded gill and cave are out of bounds. Across a simple footbridge a path goes left to climb to a stile leaving the gill as quickly as you entered it. A winding green track climbs the pasture above to a gate onto open fell at a limekiln.

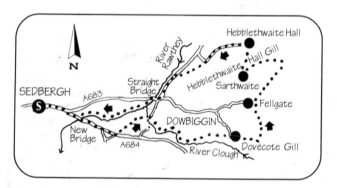

Turn left along a track above the intake wall, crossing Dovecote Gill at the head of its secret ravine before continuing along the base of Baugh Fell. A spell away from the wall sees you near it again at Fellgate Farm, whose dogs may encourage a wide berth! Another corner is then cut to run by an old limekiln. On the brow behind - as the track forsakes the wall once more - a supreme moment awaits, with the wooded course of Hebblethwaite Hall Gill backed by an uninterrupted Howgills panorama. It is easiest to work back down to the wall as it approaches the gill, passing by shakeholes to arrive at a gate that will take you off the fell.

Before that, however, the highlight of the walk beckons, in the scarred wall of the twisted ravine just ahead. The ravine of Hebblethwaite Hall Gill is superbly sited where the gill vacates the bare moor for the rich woodland. This is a stunning locale in the Dent Fault country, the gorge carved through walls of slabby rock. Its wonders can be ideally sampled by stepping out along the projecting rib immediately in front - truly a place to linger!

Hebblethwaite Hall Gill, looking to the Howgill Fells

On resuming, go through the gate and make use of the raised bank heading away. As the thin green way fades, press on along the brow of the pasture, with your objective of Hebblethwaite Hall high across the gill. Beyond an old gateway the path drops left to trail around the perimeter of the pasture by the buildings at Sarthwaite, though the immediate goal is a pair of gateposts down to the right. From them plunge straight down into the trees. Hebblethwaite Hall Woods are in the capable hands of the Woodland Trust, which welcomes visitors. **A path descends steeply to a footbridge, and a similar re-ascent leads to a field crossing to arrive at the entrance to Hebblethwaite Hall.**

Go left on the farm drive, and when it eventually goes sharp right, take a gate on the left to maintain a straight line along the hedge to approach Ghyllas. On joining the drive, go just yards right to locate a path along the side of a garage, briefly through trees to descend to the A683. Accommodating verges lead down past sidelined Burntmill Bridge to cross the Rawthey at Straight Bridge. Across the bridge a stile begins the final leg, a simple, attractive riverside stroll. At once there is added interest as the Clough pours in for a major confluence, ending its days with a flourish in the form of a low waterfall. Doubled in power, the Rawthey returns you to New Bridge.

WINDER & CROOK

START *Sedbergh*   *Grid ref. SD 658921*

DISTANCE *4 miles/6½km*

ORDNANCE SURVEY MAPS
1:50,000
Landranger 97 - Kendal to Morecambe
Landranger 98 - Wensleydale & Upper Wharfedale
1;25,000
Explorer OL19 - Howgill Fells/Upper Eden Valley

ACCESS *Start from the town centre. Two central car parks.*
Infrequent bus links with Kendal, Kirkby Stephen and Dent.

A classic round of 'Sedbergh's Summits'. These southernmost tops of the Howgills exhibit characteristics to be found throughout the group, and form a splendid introduction to the Howgill Fells.

S   **Leave the main street by Joss Lane rising past the main car park. It swings up to the right:** *'to the fell'* **signs ease the way out of town. From its demise at a gate a farm road to Hill takes over, while your way slants to the top corner of a field. A path climbs with Settlebeck Gill to gain the open fell at a quaint old gate. With a choice of paths, take the less obvious one, running down to ford the beck above a waterfall.**

The steep slope behind conceals a sunken track to the corner of the intake wall. Now locate the good pathway sloping to the right, through bracken across the face of Crook. The course of a pipeline from Ashbeck Gill, it is impeccably graded throughout. Soon after swinging left above Ashbeck Gill, a fork is reached: take the sunken way climbing left, and as it peters out the cairn atop Crook will be quickly gained, up to the left. At 1510ft/460m, Crook's top offers sweeping views over Garsdale and the valley of the Rawthey backed by Baugh Fell, while its summit cairn brings a sighting of the Lakeland Fells. A shelter stands just to the north of the cairn.

The summit of Crook

Both Winder and parent fell Arant Haw can also be appraised now, and with a bee-line out of the question, the way to Winder is an initially pathless march. Traverse across towards Settlebeck Gill, gaining a little height to cross its marshy beginnings and a parallel path. A gentle rise will then intercept the broad Sedbergh-Calf bridleway on the ridge descending from Arant Haw. Turning your back on the higher Howgills, double back left on this green carpet. Ignoring any branches scale the broad ridge, an easy stroll on grassy knolls to Winder's Ordnance Survey column and cairn.

The superb panorama from this neat 1551ft/473m top includes a fine prospect up to the Lune Gorge and the less frequented western Howgills. Garsdale and Dentdale are both particularly appealing as they burrow deep into the higher fells of the Dales. Drop a little towards Sedbergh for an intimate bird's-eye picture, a fitting scene as Winder is popularly regarded as the town's own 'special' fell. **Leave by a path striking west towards the Lune, an outstanding green way that descends to within yards of the intake wall. Turn left to find a narrow path through bracken, meeting up with the wall as Sedbergh appears ahead. At a gate behind Lockbank Farm, drop down to a short green way into the yard, emerging via the farm drive (permissive path) onto Howgill Lane, then left to finish.**

4

BRIGFLATTS & DENT FOOT

START *Sedbergh*   *Grid ref. SD 658921*

DISTANCE *5½ miles/9km*

ORDNANCE SURVEY MAPS
1:50,000
Landranger 97 - Kendal to Morecambe
Landranger 98 - Wensleydale & Upper Wharfedale
1:25,000
Explorer OL2 - Yorkshire Dales South/West (tiny section)
Explorer OL19 - Howgill Fells/Upper Eden Valley

ACCESS *Start from the town centre. Two central car parks. Infrequent bus links with Kendal, Kirkby Stephen and Dent.*

A delightful stroll by riverbanks and gentle pastures where the rivers Rawthey and Dee merge below Sedbergh.

S Go west along the main street to the parish church and turn down the Dent road. Take the first path off to the right, a snicket that runs past the churchyard and on above Sedbergh School's cricket pitch. Meeting a track at the end, bear left on a still surfaced path along the back of the pavilion.

Cross straight over a drive to a kissing-gate into a field. Passing the frontage of the school on the right, head straight down to join the back road. Cross straight over and away along a track past more sports fields. Reaching a barn, take a kissing-gate on the right, and a path crosses to the far end of the field. Curving round beneath a lone house, it meets the Dales Way path climbing from the riverbank, running along to the right to join a narrow lane.

Follow this left past the attractive cottages at Birks (one with a 1762 datestone), but before reaching Birks Mill take a stile on the right and take the left-hand path across the field. It runs on to the far corner and straight on a further field. Then bear right to a stile and gate crossing a track and on again towards an underpass in the railway embankment ahead. To the right the embankment transforms into a cutting to approach Sedbergh's station on this former Ingleton-Tebay branch line. **Across, bear left to a ladder-stile then through two fields to emerge into the tiny settlement of Brigflatts.**

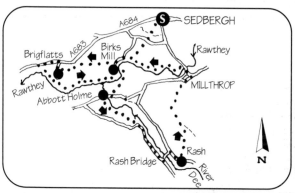

Directly opposite is a Quaker burial ground with its lines of plain headstones. Just yards to the left in the beautiful setting of this former weaving hamlet is an historic Friends' Meeting House. Incorporating a 1675 datestone, it is one of the oldest Quaker establishments in the country, and is still put to its original use. If it is open take a few respectful minutes to view the atmospheric interior of this superb old place of worship, and perhaps leave a donation. High Brigflatts, opposite, bears a 1743 datestone.

Return along the lane onto the A683. Go left for just a few minutes then take a stile on the left. A path (the Dales Way) doubles back to run above a wooded bank of the Rawthey, dropping down at the rear of Brigflatts Farm to join the riverbank, to which it tightly clings to arrive back at Birks Mill. En route, the river scenery is of the highest order, with several additional features of interest. After passing along the back of Brigflatts an old railway bridge is met: this single-arched iron structure now looks strangely out of place. To the north Winder is particularly well seen, as it is from so much of this walk. One field further and in a beautiful corner we encounter the delightful, tree-shrouded confluence of the inflowing river Dee before reaching Birks Mill. This former cotton spinning mill has for some time operated as an animal feeds mill.

Cross the Rawthey by a high footbridge in a hugely attractive section of the river. Up the small bank opposite, turn downstream. From a corner stile the path runs through the woodland of Elysian Shades, quickly climbing to a stile out of the trees. With the river gone, head away to take the first stile/gate on the right. Emerging onto Sedbergh's new golf course, watch for flying balls and follow marker posts to a gateway opposite, then continue away to a stile onto another narrow lane.

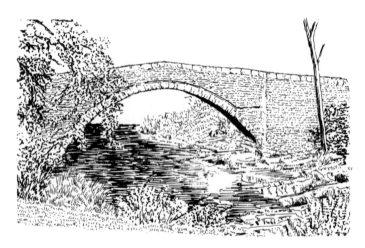

Abbott Holme Bridge

Go right just as far as Abbott Holme Bridge, then take a stile on the left. This admits to another section of the disjointed golf course. This time be especially wary of balls flying over from the left: here the sportsmen must hit their ball over the river Dee, or forfeit it to the foaming waters! This again is a lovely section of river, the Dee passing beneath its shapely final bridge prior to being swallowed up by the Rawthey.

Head upstream on a sketchy path, quickly escaping the golf course. Beyond a tiny stream the route bears left along the line of a rising field boundary. At the end a stile admits to rougher pasture, and a clear, thin trod. This slants gently up the steepening bank above the river to find a ladder-stile in the wall at the top.

Crossing this stile is a fine moment as Dentdale is revealed ahead, yet with all the earlier features still present. This super prospect of the river is backed by the Howgills, with the massive hills of Baugh Fell, Rise Hill and Whernside on offer, and Combe Scar overlooking the foot of Dentdale. **A delectable green way heads off above a dense bracken bank, tracing the wall all the way on to reach a stile by sheep pens onto a back lane. Go left along this traffic-free lane with its grassy central strip.** The surroundings of the nearby river remain idyllic. The first buildings reached are an old mill - with some millstones still lined up outside - and Dent Foot Methodist Chapel, a humble place of worship. **Just beyond, at Rash Bridge, cross the river and climb to the Dent road.**

Go right just as far as the farm buildings of Rash. En route you pass a white milestone, S2 referring to the distance to Sedbergh. **Take a gate on the left and a thin path climbs to a wall-corner, continuing up to a stile: this is the only real climb of the walk. Continue up the next field, bearing left to find a ladder-stile at the top corner. This admits to a lovely green bridleway. Go left, and at an early fork remain on the top one which soon swings round to the right to the brow.** This high point of the walk sees you trade Dentdale for the Rawthey scene once more, as Sedbergh and the inimitable Howgill Fells return.

The Howgill Fells from the old golf course above Millthrop

A stile admits onto the old golf course. Go straight ahead, crossing a track which is soon rejoined and followed away. This soon heads more steeply downhill, becoming a stony lane to descend into

Millthrop. Turn right through the hamlet to a T-junction. Millthrop is a tiny, tightly packed mill settlement, featuring an attractive terrace of old millworkers' cottages and a curiously shaped Methodist chapel of 1888. **Go left at the junction to drop back onto the Dent road alongside the Rawthey, just short of Millthrop Bridge.**

Morning mist leaving Winder, from Bruce Loch

Cross the bridge and unless desperate to finish, take a kissing-gate after a drive on the left. Bear right around the field and take a gate into the wood at the far end. The path soon swings right at a curious walled trench before leaving the wood. Go left with the fence, passing right of a small ruin to drop down the field towards the Rawthey. Head upstream a short way, passing the nature reserve of Bruce Loch before the path rises towards a house. Here turn right to retrace the outward route back into town.

Friends' Meeting House, Brigflatts

5

FROSTROW FELLS

START Sedbergh   Grid ref. SD 658921

DISTANCE 6¾ miles/11km

ORDNANCE SURVEY MAPS
1:50,000
Landranger 97 - Kendal to Morecambe (barely)
Landranger 98 - Wensleydale & Upper Wharfedale
1:25,000
Explorer OL2 - Yorkshire Dales South/West
Explorer OL19 - Howgill Fells/Upper Eden Valley

ACCESS Start from the town centre. Either of the two central car parks are adequate, but a start from the lay-by at New Bridge (where the road to Hawes crosses the Rawthey) is more satisfactory. Infrequent bus links with Kendal, Kirkby Stephen and Dent.

Splendid mountain scenery from the feet of two valleys.

S   **New Bridge is reached by heading east along the main street and branching right on the Hawes road at the edge of town. Cross the bridge and remain on the main road.** On the left you pass the former pinfold (once used for collecting stray farm animals) by a caravan site entrance. **At the first junction go right along the narrow lane, ignoring branches left and then right to continue along the 'no through road' that is Frostrow Lane.**

Frostrow is a widely scattered farming community devoid of a nucleus. A small Methodist chapel stands on the main road a little further east. **The lane heads past several farms to eventual demise alongside High Side Farm, and a stile ahead empties onto the Frostrow Fells.** Frostrow's straggling lane has given fine prospects of the Howgills, which broaden on gaining the open fell. Frostrow

Fells are the expanse of rough moorland forming the final barrier between Garsdale and Dentdale. Eastwards the ridge exerts itself to climb to Rise Hill.

Follow the track heading away along a minor ridge, with the dome of Rise Hill as a guide. Beyond a nearby wall corner and barn, a wall corner is reached above Holebeck Gill. The improved way rises as a sunken track above the beck, as it peters out a slim trod takes up the running to slant up to the wall on the watershed. On first joining the ridge-wall, Whernside, Great Coum and Middleton Fell appear across the deep trough of Dentdale. Part-way along is a brief view of Dent from the highest point of the walk at a modest 950ft/290m. On a grander scale, a clear day reveals the Coniston and Langdale Fells.

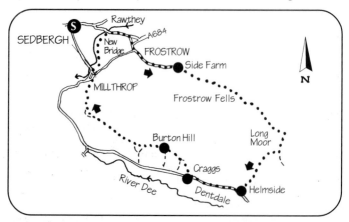

Head left with the wall as far as a stile, and take the green wallside track bound for Dentdale. This is vacated, however, at the first stile in it, to shadow another wall heading away. To the right is the shapely knoll of Helms Knott. **Through a gate the way steepens towards the valley bottom, a track forming to lead through a gate at the bottom left corner of this large enclosure. Continuing down to Helmside, use a gate on the right to pass the farm and emerge onto the road.** Helmside is the home of a crafts centre, with coffee shop. **Turn right along the valley road for three-quarters of a mile.** This road walk gives a chance to appraise the often shadowy Combe Scar across the dale. Lower Dentdale is an area of rich pastures, about which are dotted a refreshingly large number of farms.

Leave the road at the second cluster of buildings: Craggs Farm is **readily identifiable as it is entirely on the left side of the road. Take the gate opposite and head up to a stile in the adjacent wall, then slant up to Leakses. Passing in front of the farmhouse go left to a gate by the farthest barn, then cross several fields, rising slightly to Burton Hill Farm. Pass between the buildings up to an ornate gate, then cross the field bottom before aiming for Hewthwaite, the next farm. From a stile by the nearest barn, cross to a stile below a gate opposite, to cross two further fields to emerge onto the drive to Gap Farm by way of an almost hidden stile.**

Pass along the front of the house, over a field and along the foot of Gap Wood. Enclosed for much of the way, a superb green track leaves the trees behind to round the ridge end towards Sedbergh. At an early fork remain on the top one which soon swings round to the right. This brow sees you trade Dentdale for the Rawthey scene once more, as Sedbergh and the Howgill Fells return to view.

A stile admits onto the old golf course. Go straight ahead, crossing a track which is soon rejoined and followed away. This soon heads more steeply downhill, becoming a stony lane to descend into Millthrop. Turn right through the hamlet to a T-junction. Millthrop is a tiny, tightly packed mill settlement, featuring an attractive terrace of millworkers' cottages and a curiously shaped Methodist chapel of 1888. **Go left at the junction to drop back onto the Dent road alongside the Rawthey, just short of Millthrop Bridge. Cross this and go left to follow the roadside pathway back into town.** For New Bridge take a stile on the right to head upstream. The way clings to the riverbank for a grand finish.

Millthrop Bridge

25

6

FOX'S PULPIT & RIVER LUNE

START *Lowgill*   *Grid ref. SD 616965*

DISTANCE *7½ miles/12km*

ORDNANCE SURVEY MAPS
1:50,000
Landranger 97 - Kendal to Morecambe
1:25,000
Explorer OL19 - Howgill Fells/Upper Eden Valley

ACCESS *Start from the staggered crossroads just above the defunct viaduct on the B6257, 1½ miles south of the A685 junction. Parking spaces on the roadside. This corner is also known as Beck Foot.*

Firbank Fell offers glorious panoramas of the Howgills, while the return leg shadows the Lune along their base. The profusion of farms on the walk should not induce panic - only two yards are entered.

S Lowgill is known, if at all, as the site of a one time railway junction. Trains leaving the viaduct on the line from Clapham would enter Lowgill station to join the main line. Just above, motorway traffic and express trains now thunder in parallel into the Lune Gorge. **Leave the staggered crossroads by the minor road rising up past the phone box, leaving it almost at once by a short drive to a house on the left. An enclosed way rises up past the front of the house, and at a sharp bend where waymarks entice the Dales Way straight ahead, keep faith with the hedge to follow this sunken way left up to High House.**

Turn left down through the farmyard, passing the farthest buildings to a rough lane rising away. At the top keep straight on up the pathless field, following the left-hand wall over two stiles and then down to

cross a marshy little stream. At the very point where stream and wall meet, a stile conveys to the other side to follow another sunken way up to the Firbank Fell road. Turn briefly uphill for an undulating stride along its near traffic-free course. The western Howgills dominate the walk, most impressively so during this march along the fell road. The Calf, as ever, sits back unobtrusively from its kin. Enjoy also views down the Lune Valley as far as the Bowland moors. **Before long the route arrives at Fox's Pulpit.**

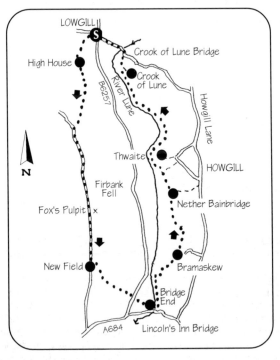

Unassuming Firbank Fell is a place of pilgrimage by virtue of the windswept corner known as Fox's Pulpit. Here, in 1652, and fresh from his vision on Pendle Hill, George Fox addressed a multitude and thus began the Quaker movement. Adjacent to a memorial tablet (see overleaf) is a tiny graveyard where a church once stood. This is an evocative spot that will cause many to lift their eyes heavenwards.

At Fox's Pulpit, Firbank Fell

On resuming, the road declines gradually to pass a house on the left, and at the next cluster (New Field) turn left along a rough lane. At its early demise slant half-right across to a gate, then straight down the fieldsides to enter a larger, sloping pasture. Just below a wall corner on the left is a short row of trees, which can be followed down to a stile into Hawkrigg Wood. A lovely path slants down this all-too-brief woodland interlude.

Lincoln's Inn Bridge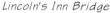

On emerging, shapely Winder appears across the Lune. **Maintain the slant left to a field corner, below which is a gate onto the B6257. Cross straight over and on a short-lived path over the brow to drop down to the farm at Lincoln's Inn Bridge.** Not surprisingly, this was once a hostelry, and recalls the name of a former landlord. **With a wary eye on traffic cross the bridge, and from a gate on the left commence the long return up the Lune.**

Approaching the Lune Viaduct

Through several stiles along the charming riverbank the old Lune Viaduct soon appears, with Crosdale Beck being forded to reach it. If in spate, an alternative is to turn up the near side of the wall, under a rail bridge and up by the stream to reach Low Branthwaite. The red sandstone and metal arches loom in dramatic fashion above a pastoral scene, no doubt startling the lambs when Lowgill-Clapham trains thundered over: in recent times the 'sport' of bungee-jumping has been witnessed here.

The way passes under the tall arches before rising up the field. The path swings right then fades before crossing to a stile, from where a track heads away with the parallel beck to Low Branthwaite. Cross the farm road to a stile opposite, and follow the left-hand fence away. Rising up the field you become briefly enclosed: emerging, cross to a gap-stile to the left of Bramaskew Farm, straight ahead. From the vicinity of Bramaskew the church at Firbank is easily located, directly below our route over the fell. Also prominent on several occasions is the grassy line of the old railway across the Lune.

Continue on to another stile, and down a large field to a small barn. A track commences, becoming enclosed to lead to Nether Bainbridge. Without entering its confines take a stile on the left, passing the rear of a barn then going left with the facing wall. Use a gate at a bend to climb to a little brow, then on to descend to Hole House Farm. Entering its yard, bear left along the private-looking way between dwellinghouses to a gate. A footbridge crosses Smithy Beck and the lower path leads down to a stile. Now cross to accompany the Lune through a large pasture below Thwaite Farm. Here you encounter the river at close quarters, its wide, stony bank leading the eye to Fell Head, westernmost 2000-footer of the Howgills.

A footbridge crosses Chapel Beck and the river remains in close company as far as a gate below Crook of Lune Farm up to the right. This final section is a lovely riverbank ramble, with the part-wooded

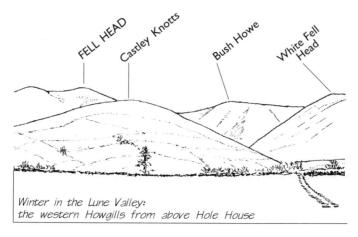

FELL HEAD   Castley Knotts   Bush Howe   White Fell Head

Winter in the Lune Valley:
the western Howgills from above Hole House

*Crook of Lune Bridge,
with Fell Head behind*

bank being rich in springtime flora. **Follow the track away to join a narrow road descending to Crook of Lune Bridge.** This is a truly beautiful structure, curving at each end and then inclining to a narrow crest. Dating possibly from almost 500 years ago, it fortunately carries only local traffic - yet is within half a mile of the M6. **Across it, a short steep climb concludes the walk by passing beneath the arches of Lowgill Viaduct.**

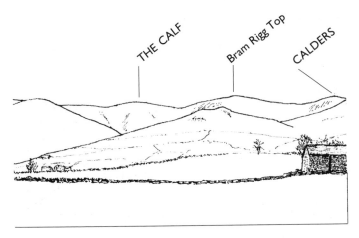

7

BRAM RIGG & ARANT HAW

START *Howgill*   *Grid ref. SD 633950*

DISTANCE *7½ miles/12km*

ORDNANCE SURVEY MAPS
1:50,000
Landranger 97 - Kendal to Morecambe
Landranger 98 - Wensleydale & Upper Wharfedale
1:25,000
Explorer OL19 - Howgill Fells/Upper Eden Valley

ACCESS *Howgill church is 2¾ miles along Howgill Lane out of Sedbergh, sat in a hollow behind a gated road. There is room for thoughtful parking alongside. A modest donation in the collecting box inside this lovely church would be a nice gesture for the use of the verge. Squeezing vehicles into the passing places and verges of Howgill Lane is likely to obstruct local traffic.*

Outstanding green pathways on archetypal Howgill slopes present a magnificent circuit over the western Howgill Fells.

S Dating from 1838, the homely church of the Holy Trinity stands beside Chapel Beck, and is the heart of Howgill's scattered farming community. **Back on Howgill Lane, turn right, steeply uphill to the drive to Blandsgill. From an adjacent stile head up the fieldsides by Smithy Beck to a gate into the yard at Birkhaw. Turn left past the buildings and a broad track heads away, along a couple of fieldsides then left at the end, on a wallside to a gate onto the open fell.**

Heading away, the track slowly curves away from the wall beneath the knoll of Seat Knott and drops down to ford Swarth Greaves Beck and Bram Rigg Beck either side of a sheepfold. Climbing the

other side bear right at a junction, and a slanting climb ensues up the flank of Seevy Rigg. The way eases at a sheepfold on a level section of the ridge. The upper half of the ascent scales Bram Rigg proper, passing through rock cuttings before a prolonged but highly enjoyable pull towards Bram Rigg Top. As the going eases the way traverses left above the head of Calf Beck, and runs on to a saddle where it meets the main Calf path coming from Sedbergh.

A visit to the summit of the Calf is optional, as the continuing route turns right here. However, it is but minutes away to the left, just a short final pull to the Ordnance Survey column. At 2218ft/676m, this marks the summit of the Howgill Fells: see also WALK 1.

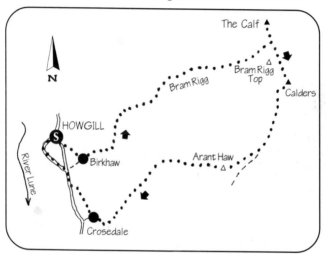

Leave by heading south on the Sedbergh path, and back in the first depression keep on past the route of ascent and remain on the main path: a brief diversion gently right, however, will lead to the unglamorous summit of Bram Rigg Top. Though merely a shoulder of the Calf, Bram Rigg Top (2204ft/672m) is so near it may as well be included: seek out its cairn of half a dozen stones!

The main path continues south to very quickly reach the cairn on Calders. At 2211ft/674m this superbly sited summit is a fine vantage point, resting on the edge of a more pronounced drop than the principal summit.

From the fence corner just beyond, the broad path descends steeply to a saddle, then along the neck of Rowantree Grains (leaving the fence behind) to rise to a shoulder of Arant Haw. Just short of the brow leave the main path, and a thinner one bears gently right up to Arant Haw's meagre cairn at 1985ft/605m.

This stage enjoys glorious views to the right of the western cirque of high Howgills, from shapely Fell Head around to Calders (note that the Calf itself is now hidden behind Bram Rigg Top). More distantly, the long Lakeland skyline features Black Combe, the Coniston Fells, the Scafells and Great Gable, and the Helvellyn group over Ill Bell and High Street.

Arant Haw from the south-west, with Winder in front

Resume westwards to commence the descent on a delightful grassy path down the gentle ridge. Outspread ahead is the Lune Valley, with the redundant Lowgill Viaduct prominent. Reaching a saddle in front of a grassy knoll the path becomes faint, and forks. Keep left, descending the south-westerly spur of Nab on an intermittent path. On the steeper final section, aim for the farm and trees at Crosedale below. Deflected left by a wall corner, a track is met above Crosdale Beck. This zigzags down to cross the stream by a set of sheep pens, then slants up to a gate off the fell. The stream crossing makes for a pleasant final linger, with some aggressively rocky walls immediately downstream.

Don't advance to the cottage at Craggstone, but bear right down the edge of the trees above the delightful stream lined by some sturdy oaks. The thin path soon drops down to a footbridge on

Crosdale Beck then slants up to Crosedale Farm. Go left through the yard, but as the track goes left again and out past the house, keep straight on through a gate in front, on a farm track heading away along a hedgeside. It runs on through a second field then becomes briefly enclosed before fading. Keep straight on to a gate ahead, joining a narrow, enclosed farm track. Go left onto Howgill Lane.

Turn right as far as a crossroads with the Birkhaw drive, and for a varied finish, take the meandering back road to the left. Up to the right, enjoy a fine picture of these western Howgills, overseen by Fell Head. Across the valley, the M6 traffic appears to be using the Lowgill Viaduct!

At Howgill, looking to Bram Rigg and Calders

Ignoring all branches left, the back road winds round to drop down to Mill House. The former mill stands alongside: note the long-dry water cut on the right that once supplied a waterwheel at the mill from Chapel Beck. The church, and thus the finish, also appears just ahead, backed by the eternal skyline of fells.

8

FELL HEAD

START *Fairmile Gate*   *Grid ref. SD 629978*

DISTANCE *7¼ miles/11½ km*

ORDNANCE SURVEY MAPS
1:50,000
Landranger 97 - Kendal to Morecambe
Landranger 98 - Wensleydale & Upper Wharfedale
1:25,000
Explorer OL19 - Howgill Fells/Upper Eden Valley

ACCESS *Fairmile Gate is on a minor road 3 miles south of the A685 at Low Borrow Bridge. It is the point where Fairmile Road leaves the open fell to become Howgill Lane. There is a roadside parking area on the brow just north of the bridge, opposite a small clump of trees.*

A steep initial ascent onto a magnificent circuit over the highest western Howgill Fells. Fellow humans only on the Calf, briefly!

S Fell Head rises directly above Fairmile Gate, set back behind the slopes of Linghaw: the start is an immediate ascent. **From the top end of the parking area a clear bracken path gently rises north of Dry Gill towards the intimidating slopes of Linghaw.** When the bracken ends enjoy a well-earned break, with super views over the Lune Valley to Grayrigg Common; with a particularly good stretch of the Lune immediately updale, as it emerges from the Lune Gorge. Far beyond is a Lakeland skyline featuring the Coniston Fells, with the Scafells' defile of Mickledore slotting neatly in further right.

This steepest section ends as a broader green way curves up to the right, then steeply again as one of several parallel grooves rise past a few scattered stones to ease out on the grassy felltop. Keep straight on over a couple of cross-trods to gain the grassy top of

Linghaw (1640ft/500m). Fell Head returns to the scene, hopefully looking much more attainable now: the summit cairn sits back to the left of the western top. Over to the left are the wilder upper recesses of Carlingill. **Follow the trod down to the intervening saddle, and again ignoring any cross-paths take the most obvious, initially broader path directly up onto Blake Ridge, the north-western spur of Fell Head. A delectable path winds invitingly up to gain the western top of Fell Head, marked by a cairn. It is now but two minutes along to the more substantial summit cairn.**

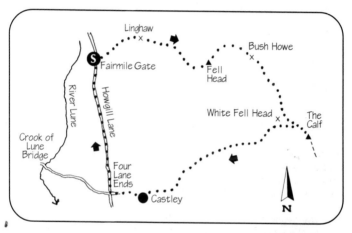

This last stage enjoys the benefits of the new view ahead to the high Calf skyline. Indeed, a particular attraction of Fell Head is that despite its natural high-level link to the main massif, it nevertheless has a very independent, detached feel to it. At 2100ft/640m this is the third of the 2000-footers and its 'outpost' situation makes it a superb all-round viewpoint, looking down on the Lune Gorge, across to the Whinfell Ridge and the skyline of Lakeland.

As a bee-line to the Calf is out of the question, leave by heading north along the broad summit ridge, the path curving round to descend to the pronounced (and only notable) saddle of Windscarth Wyke. En route, the northern Howgills ridges are well aligned striking north from the central massif: across them are the rounded, even less frequented tops of the Hazelgill Knott and Randygill Top-Yarlside ridges.

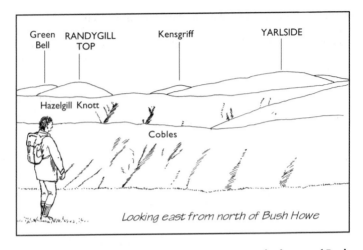

Green Bell   RANDYGILL TOP   Kensgriff   YARLSIDE

Hazelgill Knott

Cobles

Looking east from north of Bush Howe

A steeper pull ends abruptly on the grassy, unmarked crest of Bush Howe at 2044ft/623m. Remain on the main ridge path as it rises gently to the waiting trig. point on the Calf, absorbing the main White Fell path and concluding with a short final pull. During this stage a branch bears right to visit the highest, indiscernible point of White Fell Head (2100ft/640m). If not visiting the Calf then this is the way to go, for it runs increasingly thinly on past a summit pool to meet the descent path. At 2218ft/676m the Calf is the highest point in the entire group: see also WALK 1.

Fell Head from White Fell

Leave the Calf by the same path, for just a couple of minutes, but this time keep left on the broader White Fell path as it curves around the head of Calf Beck. After a steady warm-up, the path begins a smashing descent of the grassy rib of White Fell. En route, a hoary cairn just over to the right merits a detour for the view it reveals of the 'Horse of Busha', a mile north on Bush Howe: this is simply a natural arrangement of scattered stones which resemble the shape of a horse. The cairn also serves as a rare and useful shelter. **The green track's gentle descent of the long spur culminates at a ford on Long Rigg Beck, then curves up beneath Castley Knotts.**

Pause here to look back at the fairest of scenes, with the western ridges of the Calf's entourage interlocking between deep-cut side becks. Of the similarly appointed tops, it is the Calf itself that, surprisingly, appears of least significance. Truly this is God's own country. **The track runs to a gate off the fell, now enclosed to quickly reach Castley Farm in its entirely enviable setting.**

Keep straight on the farm drive, passing Cookson's Tenement and out onto a crossroads at Four Lane Ends. Turn right along Howgill Lane, remaining on this to return to Fairmile Gate. Sandwiched between hedgerows this mile and a half on tarmac is a pleasant conclusion, being virtually traffic-free and enjoying excellent views of the circuit just completed. On descending to the cattle-grid that long since replaced the gate, note the old milestone on the right advising the distances to Kendal and Orton. The Fairmile Road was, much earlier, on the Roman road leading to the camp at Low Borrow Bridge.

Fell Head, looking to The Calf

9

CARLINGILL & BLACK FORCE

START *Carlingill Bridge*   *Grid ref. SD 624995*

DISTANCE *4½ miles/7km*

ORDNANCE SURVEY MAPS
1:50,000
Landranger 97 - Kendal to Morecambe
1:25,000
Explorer OL19 - Howgill Fells/Upper Eden Valley

ACCESS *Start from a popular roadside parking area on the unfenced Fairmile Road, just south of the bridge.*

The hidden ravines of Carlingill are the fascinating objectives of this highly memorable little expedition. The Spout and Black Force are two remarkable, aptly named physical features secreted in the folds of the gill.

S Single-arched Carlingill Bridge was very much the final outpost of Yorkshire's West Riding. The 'Fair Mile' is the road's open stretch south of the bridge - it is too. **From Carlingill Bridge turn to follow the beck up its enclosed course, a clear path materialising to remain largely evident all the way. The hills increasingly close in, and at the second inflowing gill on the right (Small Gill), the valley narrows markedly.**

With no obvious means of progress, cross to the opposite bank. A rough wall of scree tumbles to the deeply carved gill, but after a brief pull a surprise path is found to traverse cautiously across. Its return to the floor of the gill coincides with the spectacular moment of arrival at the foot of the ravine of Black Force.

Black Force is a series of tumbling little falls throughout the full length of a dark walled ravine. The confluence here is a situation to savour, and indeed to take stock of the next stage. Two options await, and if that last section has given enough excitement then a direct route crosses the left-hand (main) beck to commence a steep pull up the inviting rib on the left side of Black Force's ravine. **If bound for further thrills and spills, keep faith with the floor of Carlin Gill. Initially there seems no obvious way again, but a trodden path soon forms to clamber its way along the right-hand (south) bank.**

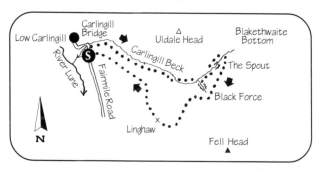

Passing a lovely waterslide this absorbing path is halted all too soon at the impasse of the Spout. The Spout is a stunning waterfall that is not fully seen until penetrating to the limit of exploration. Well named, it pours as if from a major leak into its colourful amphitheatre.

Escape comes by crossing the beck to a choice of a steep, stony pull or a cleaner scramble up tilted rock: either demands caution, while the latter earns an even more intimate view of the Spout. On the flank above, continue up steep grass to a level trod that lends itself to a stroll along to the hollow of Blakethwaite Bottom. After the claustrophobia of Carlin Gill, the basin of Blakethwaite Bottom is a contrastingly spacious upland. **Cross the thin branch of the beck to a clearer path opposite, there doubling back to cross the main arm of the beck (Great Ulgill Beck). Now take the upper of two slender ways heading off across the grass, rising just a little before aiming for the unmistakable head of Black Force.**

The mercurial path returns high above the gorge of upper Carlin Gill to arrive at the calm upper reaches above Black Force. Across Little Ulgill Beck the main path makes a short climb, while a lower

alternative slants more gently across to the rough terrain at the head of the ravine, a most dramatic vantage point. **Back on the upper path, it rounds this north shoulder of Fell Head and sets forth on a wonderful traverse around to a col linking the minor top of Linghaw with its parent fell.** This elevated return leg is along the upper flanks of Fell Head, one of the Howgills' five 2000ft mountains (see WALK 8). Grand views range from the high peaks of central Lakeland to the waters of Morecambe Bay.

The Spout, Carlingill

At this neat crossroads of green ways turn right to surmount the grassy brow of Linghaw (1640ft/500m) and then slope gently north-west down to a useful trod. With the Lune Gorge outspread below the finish is an obvious one, tracing the long shoulder of the fell back to the start. Sketchy in places, the breaks in the path can be easily linked up, though in practise this is of little consequence.

(10)

BORROWDALE

START *Low Borrowbridge*   *Grid ref. NY 606014*

DISTANCE *7¼ miles/11½ km*

ORDNANCE SURVEY MAPS
1:50,000
Landranger 91 - Appleby-in-Westmorland
1:25,000
Explorer OL7 - English Lakes South East
Explorer OL19 - Howgill Fells/Upper Eden Valley

ACCESS *Start from a good parking area just off the A685, at the staggered junction before it crosses Borrow Beck. Alternative starts: Lune's Bridge or Salterwath Bridge.*

The lovely Lune Gorge shrugs off man's insults, while wild Borrowdale is a stolen chunk of Lakeland.

S **A gentle start leads into the heart of Borrowdale, heading through the gate and following the initially surfaced farm road up the valley.** The start is made pleasanter still by the presence of Borrowdale Wood, which contains a fine deciduous mixture. **The ensuing rough road crosses Borrow Beck and runs to the farm of Low Borrowdale.** Sat in happy seclusion, it is the only farm in the six miles of the valley between the A6 and Low Borrow Bridge.

Appropriately enough, Low Borrowdale has the look of a Lakeland farmstead, for the valley itself, locked in a no-man's-land between Dales and Lakes, exhibits a greater affinity with the eastern valleys of the latter. Indeed, Borrowdale starts out within the Lakes' boundary, though tourists know only one Borrowdale! It was, however, sufficiently beautiful to attract the covetous eyes of the water authorities not so long ago - they didn't get it though.

Take the gate to the left of the house and at once forsake the valley track by doubling back up one to the right. It climbs above the farm and through a couple of fields onto the open fell. On the very verge of the ridge-top on Roundthwaite Common the way suddenly expires: head straight on through the grassy saddle and drop down to the marshy beginnings of **Burn Gill**. Semi-wild ponies graze these parts, while the very fortunate might glimpse a 'Haweswater' eagle wheeling high over Borrowdale.

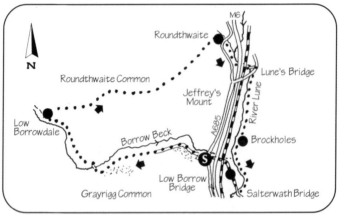

Keeping left of the beck, a sketchy way drops down again to meet a track coming in from the left. This swings round, parallel with the beck down to the right, to falter on wet ground before re-appearing at a patch of bracken to wind down to cross the beck. All is now clear as a broad track heads away, being joined by a wall and eventually descending to the farming hamlet of Roundthwaite.

A green track swings right to meet the narrow road, turning right for just a few yards before dropping down to pick up a thin path by Roundthwaite Beck. This is shadowed through its final yards to a confluence with the Lune, just prior to the motorway bridge. Here the right of way climbs to a stile in the fence above, then up the fieldside to another stile back onto the Roundthwaite road, joining the elevated A685 to cross motorway, railway and river to find **Lune's Bridge on the left.** Walkers regularly make use of an anglers' path accompanying the Lune under the bridges to rise to a stile at the road-end at Lune's Bridge, though it is not a public right of way.

With road, railway and latterly motorway joining the river Lune in its squeeze through the gorge, this is an animated scene in the midst of an otherwise remote location. It was the stealthy northward encroachment of the M6 in 1970 that brought greatest upheaval, the end result being that both Low Borrow and Lune's Bridges were made virtually redundant, the latter entirely so. The endless whine of traffic cannot ruin this fair scene, however, for the stranded bridge strides as always over the Lune as it funnels through a narrow ravine. The grassy terrace atop the gorge makes a suitable spot for a sojourn.

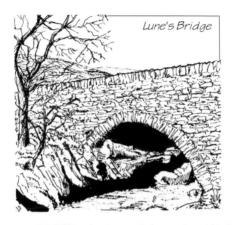

Lune's Bridge

Just above Lune's Bridge the A685 is crossed to head down-river on the Brockholes farm road, running high above the Lune. At the cattle-grid just before the isolated farm take a gate on the right, crossing the small, rough enclosure to the right end of the buildings. Pass along the outside on the steep bank above the river, at the end dropping down to gain the bank of the Lune. It is now simply a case of strolling downstream. Borrow Beck's confluence with the Lune is well seen during this section. **The stroll concludes with a woodland path onto the road at Salterwath Bridge.** The bridge is a local rarity in that it still retains its purpose!

Cross the bridge, rising past the farm at Low Borrow Bridge. The old main road comes in here. Unmistakable at Low Borrow Bridge is the elevated mound of a Roman fort, a small camp on the road north to Brougham, near Penrith. **Final encounters with railway and motorway brings you back to the A685 almost opposite the start.**

11

BRETHERDALE

START *Greenholme*   *Grid ref. NY 597057*

DISTANCE *7¼ miles/11½km*

ORDNANCE SURVEY MAPS
1:50,000
Landranger 90 - Penrith, Keswick & Ambleside
Landranger 91 - Appleby-in-Westmorland
1:25,000
Explorer OL7 - English Lakes South East

ACCESS *Start from the hamlet, reached from the A685 in the Lune Gorge, or from Orton. Ample parking area by the green. Please take extra care on the narrow road from the A685 via Roundthwaite. An alternative start is the Shap Summit layby on the A6 (GR 553062).*

A real 'away from it all' walk in a true no-man's-land. Some rougher moments but generally easy, and with glorious views. And a few steps in the Lake District National Park, to boot!

S Greenholme is a tiny settlement nestling in a fold of the hills on little known Birk Beck. Its handful of houses are on or near the spacious green and the beck. A very humble Methodist church stands by the green, and a house carries a memorial tablet of 1887.

Leave by a track leaving between two buildings by the phone box. This rises through the fields to the farm buildings at Low Whinhowe. Keep right of them and on through a gate ahead. As the track swings left into trees, keep on up the fenceside on a distinct groove of some age. From a gate at the top corner steer a pathless course directly up the meadow, joining a green track running from the ruin of High Whinhowe just to the right. Cross straight over and up to a gate in the top wall, from where a rough track rises to the next gate. Advance on over open ground to meet a narrow back road.

Ahead now is a fine prospect of unfrequented Bretherdale. Its appearance is quite distinctly that of a typical valley of easternmost Lakeland: rough, lichen-covered walls, bracken flanks and the odd rock outcrop. **Cross straight over to a gate from where a super green way heads off.** This old road contours delightfully along the flank of the hill, forging into the valley. Over to the left the side valley of Breasthigh Beck forms a deep trough: the continuation of your present old road can be clearly discerned climbing up through it, from where it descends to Borrowdale to meet the old A6.

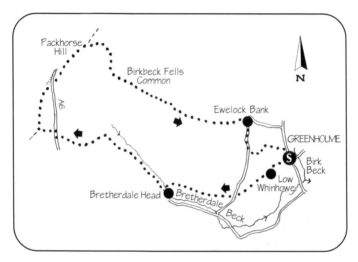

Your smashing way runs on beneath Scots Pine and bracken pastures, and through a former hedgerowed section. Towards the end, above the farm at Bretherdale Head, it drops down, part sunken and gone to seed but easy enough to negotiate. Pass down through a couple of old gates to a corner with Bretherdale Beck through the gateway below. Turn downstream a few yards to find a ford and clapper bridge. This shadowy corner is a charming spot.

Cross to a couple of barns and turn upstream, squeezing by a barn at Greenhead into a more open riverbank. Approaching an old wall rise left with it to avoid a steep, wooded bank. At the brow pause to savour a fine prospect of the secluded valley, with the beck below your steep bank, and abundant tree cover. Up to your left

47

are steep, wooded flanks beneath George Crag. **Cross to a gate in a fence from where the old bridle-track forges on, a little reedy at times but largely good and obvious. The way runs along the valley flank well above the beck, passing the ruin of Parrocks opposite (circular sheepfold below you) and on through delightful country.**

After the bank steepens again and becomes more wooded, you are deflected left by a minor stream to find an old wall. Climb the tongue between stream and wall, then on with the wall. As it turns downhill keep straight on an initially grooved way, aiming for steep sided streams just ahead. The old way curves down to meet them at the confluence. This really is a charming spot to break, with tumbling streams and a handful of native trees.

Clapper bridge,
Bretherdale Head

Crossing the streams the way is deeply incised up the opposite bank. At the top, pause to look back down the valley before moving off. Bear left a short way to pick up the route, the faint grassy line having swung sharply left to rise up the bleaker moor parallel with the tiny stream. Up ahead the knoll of Crookdale Crag is prominent: a lesser rounded one to its right is our objective, the ambitiously named Red Crag. Rising above this now sluggish beck the old way can be retained for a while, then at a broader marshy depression rise right to gain the top of Red Crag.

A few outcrops mark the crest as the ridge-wall negotiates them. Appearing rather suddenly ahead, the first sighting of the A6 is most likely a big waggon rumbling over the fells. The view reaches down the A6 corridor, with Crookdale opposite and a glimpse left down towards Borrowdale; the massive Shap Pink Quarry looms over to the right. **Go right with the wall, and just past a junction take a stile in a fence. A green path heads away through heather to descend to a stile onto the A6.**

Go right and consider two options for the next short stage. The easiest way remains on the verge of this now quiet road, passing a memorial stone, phone box, lay-bys and TV repeater station hut, to drop down to where the old road crosses it, unmissable. This point also marks the true Shap Summit, at 1397ft/426m. The A6 is a road out of which legends were born, a notoriously inhospitable highway over the fells that was, until the arrival of the motorway, the main north-south artery on this side of the Pennines. The tablet on the memorial stone sums it up:

> THIS MEMORIAL PAYS TRIBUTE TO
> THE DRIVERS AND CREWS OF VEHICLES
> WHO MADE POSSIBLE THE SOCIAL
> AND COMMERCIAL LINKS BETWEEN
> NORTH AND SOUTH ON THIS OLD AND
> DIFFICULT ROUTE OVER SHAP FELL
> BEFORE THE OPENING OF THE M6
> MOTORWAY.
>
> REMEMBERED TOO ARE THOSE WHO BUILT
> AND MAINTAINED THE ROAD AND THE
> GENERATIONS OF LOCAL PEOPLE WHO
> GAVE FREELY OF FOOD AND SHELTER
> TO STRANDED TRAVELLERS IN BAD
> WEATHER.

The alternative samples a rough section of the road that preceded the A6, here merely an abandoned green way currently in serious disrepair. Go right only as far as the first gate opposite, and a track heads away to join the old road at right-angles. Turn right on it, and beyond a bridle-gate and cross-track it runs rutted and a little too waterlogged for enjoyable progress. This brief encounter with the Lake District is indeed a forgettable one! **Soon swinging right it returns to the A6 before reaching a plantation.**

However gained, take the stile/gate on the right: a contrastingly firm track takes the old road away. It drops then rises beside a knoll on the left. This is Packhorse Hill, a dead giveaway to this route's historic past. Just past here is a junction. Leave the old road and pass through the gate on the right, from where a firm track heads away to a shooting box visible. Just before it the main track swings right at a fork (not on map). Though officially the bridleway runs to the shelter, its ensuing pathless course rises behind it to quickly rejoin the broad track: common sense would therefore suggest simply remaining on the track!

Keep on as it meanders along the watershed before starting to descend towards Bretherdale. At this stage abandon it and go left to the short pull to the cairn on the pimple of Crag Hill. This is another good spot, a minor rocky knoll with fine views and some shelter. Just before it a green track was crossed. Return to it and head right (north) to a bend where it absorbs the partly traceable true course of the bridleway from above the shooting box. Your way is easier, avoiding some aimless wandering and also enjoying a visit to Crag Hill.

Bear right from this junction and a splendid march down the fell ensues, clear and declining all the way. As your grassy trail strides down Birkbeck Fells Common, far-reaching views lead the eye over the limestone plateau to the North Pennines and around the Mallerstang fells to the Howgills. Just after a small ruin the way becomes briefly faint, but erring slightly right it picks up again and becomes a firmer modern track alongside a wall. Soon the wall turns away, keep left on the main track to drop to a firmer track. Go left to drop down again to join a back road alongside Ewelock Bank Farm.

Turn right a short way, and approaching a dip before a house and a cattle-grid with limekiln below, turn left down open ground to find a wall-stile in the corner. Here begins a delectable finish that proves a real bonus. Bear right to a fence-stile, then resume downstream with the tiny trickle (it is basically downstream all the way to the finish). A larger stream merges and leads down to a narrow gate in the bottom corner. Cross and continue down a gorse bank on a thin trod through very colourful surroundings. At the bottom corner use a wall-stile 15 yards left of the stream. Head on through a gateway and down to a sturdy wooden footbridge. Turn downstream again to a stile back onto the edge of the green.

12

BLEASE FELL
& TEBAY GILL

START Tebay   Grid ref. NY 618044

DISTANCE 6 miles/9½km

ORDNANCE SURVEY MAPS
1:50,000
Landranger 91 - Appleby-in-Westmorland
1:25,000
Explorer OL19 - Howgill Fells/Upper Eden Valley

ACCESS Start from the village centre, ample roadside parking. About half a minute off the M6! Served by infrequent buses from Kendal, Penrith and Appleby.

An uncomplicated and lonely circuit of Tebay Gill.

S Tebay is an unassuming village, for decades known only as a name on the railway map of Britain. Even that distinction has been lost, and replaced, for better or for worse, by the constant drone of the motorway and its attendant access point. The village features a Primitive Methodist Chapel of 1885, a Post office, toilets and two pubs, the central *Cross Keys* and the *Barnaby Rudge* on the Kendal road. The old school houses an activity centre that was also a youth hostel for a while. Detached from the village - as is the hamlet of Old Tebay - are rows of former railway workers' cottages, overlooking the junction of the dismantled branch to Darlington with the main line (west) to Scotland. They don't stop here any more though......

Leave Mount Pleasant at the top of the village by a road rising past the outdoor centre. It crosses a cattle-grid onto the open moor, and rises to serve several farms. The walk enjoys an immediate retrospect of the Cross Fell range beyond the Eden Valley. The whole of this open country is commonly referred to as Tebay Fell, and neither stile nor gate are to interrupt your strides. **On the brow near a wall-corner the road loses its full surface, and here take a second track branching right to rise alongside the wall.**

The track runs past farm buildings of Tebaygill, and as it starts to drop towards the beck, leave by a fork onto the grassy ridge. From here on a generally clear track scales the fell at the most generous of gradients. The pull to the knoll of Powson Knott might earn a halt to savour the Lakeland skyline beyond the lovely environs of Borrowdale, ranging from the Coniston Fells to High Street.

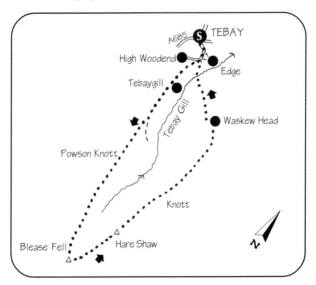

Over the brow of Powson Knott some small pools are passed. Blease Fell's summit appears ahead, with Fell Head peeping over the Hare Shaw col. Hare Shaw itself is prominent throughout the climb. The buzz of the Lune Gorge is immediately below Blease Fell's flanks. **A further knoll is topped before gaining the peaty top of Blease Fell at 1555ft/474m.** Full compensation for the absence of a cairn in this bleak spot is found in the neat structure occupying a far worthier position a little beyond: this is the place to break journey.

The valley of Carlingill from Blease Fell, with Fell Head behind

Doubling back to the left a marshy crossing to the less inspiring Hare Shaw (1548ft/372m) is quickly accomplished, bearing a little right to avoid the worst of the wet ground. From the cairn head north down the broad ridge, with a pleasant, grassy surface and an intermittent tractor track returning. The minor swelling of Knott can be topped or skirted to the left before more level terrain leads to the farm buildings of Waskew Head which have long been in view. Its access track - with grassier alternatives - leads straight down to cross Tebaygill Beck (look for the cross before it) and so meet up with the outward route for the final few minutes.

On Blease Fell, looking west to Borrowdale

13

UPPER LUNE VALLEY

START *Gaisgill*   *Grid ref. NY 645054*

DISTANCE *5 miles/8km*

ORDNANCE SURVEY MAPS
1:50,000
Landranger 91 - Appleby-in-Westmorland
1:25,000
Explorer OL19 - Howgill Fells/Upper Eden Valley

ACCESS *Start from Rayne Bridge, on the Kelleth road (this is the by-passed old road) just east of the main Gaisgill junction on the modern A685. There is a large lay-by to be found just up the hill past the bridge.*

An undemanding stroll around the upper reaches of the river Lune on the foothills of the Howgills.

❺   Rayne Bridge is a broad, long structure that once carried the main road over the already sizeable Lune. **On the upper side of the bridge take a stile on the west side (downstream) and descend to the river. Don't follow the Lune but slant to the top of the wooded bank and continue on to a gap-stile just below a gate in the wall at the end. Resume along a green terrace between trees to the next stile, then out in the open head away with a long defunct wall.** Over to the left the Howgills already look splendid.

A gentle decline leads to the next gap-stile, slightly hidden where fence and wall meet. A dead straight contour leads on to the next one, then across to a less obvious stile in a kink in the wall above a hogg-hole (a sheep 'door'). Head away with a wall to the final stile, with Raisgill Hall just below. Before the farm a hollow is passed. This pronounced circular depression is an historic cock pit, where the once very popular 'sport' of cockfighting took place, to the tune of much gambling. **Bear right into the farmyard then out onto its drive onto the road.** Look back left to see the hall itself, bearing an initialled 1707 dated lintel. **Turn right up the road.** On the left is a splendidly preserved limekiln, while Rais Beck is pleasant company on the right. Ahead, limestone heights reach to the horizon. **At a junction at the end turn right down to Fawcett Mill.**

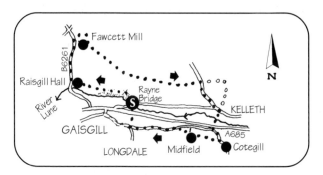

Continue past the mill turning, down to a bridge and then back up the other side. In the mill's wooded grounds down to the right, note a lovely arched footbridge almost lost in greenery, and the ruins of earlier buildings. **The traffic-free byway climbs and slowly loses its surface on the brow.** Looking back, the far eastern fells of Lakeland are now on view. **Advance on, a brief section beyond a barn being a fine green way before becoming a firmer track again.**

Descending to a junction with Waingap Lane, the route turns down to the right to a junction with the old main road on the edge of Kelleth. If still signposted, a Countryside Stewardship access scheme presents an alternative way into Kelleth, by crossing straight over and up the wallside. Reaching a fence, take advantage of this route to enjoy a cracking prospect of Yarlside peeking through the head of Bowderdale: a shapely eminence that in winter mantle looks truly stunning. At a fence turn down to a gate and then down the field to a gate onto the road at Kelleth.

Go left towards the hamlet, but at the first roadside house take a narrow snicket down to the right. Fleetingly a holloway in its lower reach, it leads quickly down to the riverbank, a fine spot. **Cross the**

sturdy footbridge and the old green way curves round to meet the main road. The house alongside is Kelleth Crossing Cottage, another reminder of the old railway.

Cross with care and down a short-lived lane to a T-junction. Go right for an even quicker finish, otherwise go left for two minutes towards Cotegill. This is a tiny farming hamlet with an attractive white-walled farmhouse on the right. **Without actually entering however, take a gate/stile set a couple of yards up to the right. This accesses a large field: slant back up to the top and follow the wall along to a gap-stile at the far end. Advance to a less obvious plank-stile in the short section of facing wall ahead, then head away with a wall on the right towards Midfield.**

Again with a short section of facing wall, take a stile and cross a small paddock to a gate by a barn. Go right the few yards down to the junction of the two houses' drives, then take a gate on the left alongside a garage. Step over the fence just behind and head to the far end of the field, where a tiny gate admits onto the narrow back lane. Go left for a few minutes to reach Longdale hamlet.

Continue just a little further towards Gaisgill, as far as the next buildings on the left. Note an 1860 datestone and little figure on the house. **Take a gate/stile into the field on the right and head straight across. From the gate at the end cross the main road with care to a gate opposite.** The road is re-aligned on the course of the old railway, and though traffic comes thick and fast, it can at least be seen approaching. **Bear left towards Rayne Bridge, using a gap-stile at the bridge-end onto the road.**

Rayne Bridge

14

ULDALE HEAD

START *Gaisgill*   *Grid ref. NY 639053*

DISTANCE *8¼ miles/13km*

ORDNANCE SURVEY MAPS
1:50,000
Landranger 91 - Appleby-in-Westmorland
Landranger 97 - Kendal to Morecambe (tiny section)
1:25,000
Explorer OL19 - Howgill Fells/Upper Eden Valley

ACCESS *Start from the by-passed old road at Gaisgill, with roadside parking just off the modern A685 which now runs for much of its time on the course of the former railway line.*

A bracing leg-stretcher through typical northern Howgills country. Access to the fells is by way of long, tapering ridges, and in between are hauntingly remote side valleys.

S   Gaisgill is a scattered farming hamlet beneath the northern slopes of the Howgills and overlooking the youthful river Lune. It was by-passed in the 1970s. It has a tiny Wesleyan Chapel of 1841, and just along the Tebay road is the attractive three-storeyed house at Gaisgill Farm.

From the bridge on Ellergill Beck at the Longdale junction just off the main road, go a few yards along the Longdale road then turn up the rough road on the right. It runs along the fieldside to the houses at Ellergill. Bear left up the narrow, cobbled way at the side of the cottage, and keep rising left past other dwellings and a set of sheep pens to join a firm track just above all the buildings. Bear right up this, leading gradually up a narrow strip of rough pasture between walls. Higher up it emerges onto the open fell, and forks.

Keep left here on the wallside. A long, gradual rise leads past the barns of Long Gills, and eventually the main track turns down to the isolated farm buildings at Low Shaw. A good track continues, however, all the way towards the wall corner ahead under Uldale End. The increasing views take in the fine lower stretch of Langdale down to the left, but on approaching the wall corner the middle section of this elongated valley is revealed, a real treat as the steep flanks fall from Langdale Knott on the left and Middleton on the right.

Near the wall corner the fading track bears right. Advance to the peaty corner and away on an improving trod. Just past here the wall drops sharply away to the valley, but keep straight on a thin but clear trod. This classic moment reveals more of Langdale, with the environs of the confluences with Uldale and Churn Gill. Above these, the long arm of Middleton rises to Simon's Seat, with the Hand Lake ridge to its right.

Set off on this splendid trod, turning the corner with your chosen course of Uldale reaching away. After a brief contour the path slants down through scree and bracken, in no hurry to join the meandering stream. Ultimately it touches the dale floor at the remains of a sheepfold. Though at times faint it never leaves you, leading delightfully on past another fold and into Blakethwaite Bottom to find the Blakethwaite Stone sat on a broad saddle.

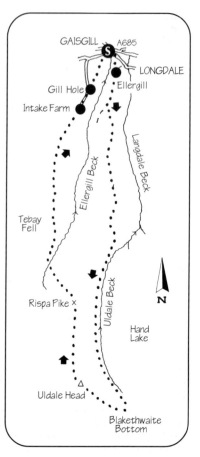

Though of modest proportions the Blakethwaite Stone is a notable landmark, bearing a benchmark, being on the old Yorkshire-Westmorland boundary, and inscribed with many initials. The saddle is actually the 'pass' between Uldale and Carlingill, ahead, though it joins the other valley from the side, rather than its head. A detour to visit the Spout (see WALK 9) can easily be accomplished.

Turn right up the grassy slopes of Uldale Head, past a few outcrops on a minor spur. The thundering sound of the Spout might be heard rising from the left. **Farmers' quad tracks can be joined on this steep slope, which soon eases to run to a substantial cairn on a grassy rib. In mist this might be taken for the summit, which waits a couple of minutes further. Here, at 1739ft/530m, a contrastingly insignificant cairn sits on a broad, inferior top.** The all-round view features the sprawling slopes of Fell Head to the south, Grayrigg Common across the Lune Valley, while to the east rises Simon's Seat. To the north gentle slopes decline to the upper Lune, with the limestone plateau behind and a distant prospect of the North Pennines.

Leave by heading north on plateau-like slopes. The objective of Rispa Pike is less than a mile distant, and another track can be picked up to lead out to it. An alternative, less peaty way is to stick to the eastern side, keeping above the steeper drop into Uldale and gaining the benefit of views therein. The ridge narrows in the slight saddle before the gentlest of rises to Rispa Pike, its top at 1555ft/474m occupied by a stone shelter above a very minor rocky knoll.

For a direct return continue down the declining ridge to meet the outward route under Uldale End. **For a completely different (but identical in character) return, strike north-west down the flank, joining a sidestream to reach a sheepfold on Eller Gill. A green track runs downstream from it, briefly, before fording the beck and slanting away up the flank of Knott. This initial surface is a grand one, and very quickly you seem to be very high above the beck.**

This same track now leads all the way back, unfailingly as it strides out down a very gently declining ridge, joining a wall and down a narrowing strip of fell - sound familiar? At Intake Farm the way becomes surfaced, leading down to the next farm buildings at Gill Hole. One can either stay on the road to finish or take a field option. **At the farm approach, as the wall rejoins, go down the right side of the wall to find a corner stile behind assorted debris. Descend the long pasture alongside a former hedge-line, passing a T-shaped sheep bield and down to a gate onto the road back in Gaisgill.**

15

SIMON'S SEAT & LANGDALE

START *Gaisgill*   *Grid ref. NY 639053*

DISTANCE *8½ miles/13½km*

ORDNANCE SURVEY MAPS
1:50,000
Landranger 91 - Appleby-in-Westmorland
1:25,000
Explorer OL19 - Howgill Fells/Upper Eden Valley

ACCESS *Start from the old road at Gaisgill, with parking just off the A685 which now runs largely on the course of the former railway line. There is also some limited parking by the old school in Longdale.*

A splendid journey into the wild recesses of magnificent Langdale, and a grand ascent and ridge walk, to boot.

S   Gaisgill is a scattered farming hamlet beneath the northern slopes of the Howgills and overlooking the youthful river Lune. It was by-passed in the 1970s. It has a tiny Wesleyan Chapel of 1841, and just along the Tebay road is the attractive three-storeyed house at Gaisgill Farm.

Head east along the back road to the farm buildings at Longdale and turn right into the hamlet. Passing the old school, keep on to the end of the tarmac at the last house on the left. Don't take a gate in front but use one on the left. A green, walled way heads away, quickly turning and slanting up the hillside. This is Cowbound Lane, an old droveway off the fells - not vehicle friendly - which remains your course for the short mile onto the fell.

Ahead, the rounded tops of your walk await. Look back to Orton's limestone heights and to the west, Lakeland's easternmost fells. **At a reedy open section remain close to the left-hand wall, the track re-forming for a final enclosed spell, increasingly pleasantly.**

At the end the track emerges onto open fell. It slants down to the right to a wall-corner then traces the wallside up to the right above a reedy stream. This remains so until fading just short of a brow, where advance to the wall corner. Revealed is an outstanding prospect of the upper recesses of Langdale, and the fells of your walk across the dale. This is the Howgills' finest valley, exuding a particular sense of wildness between shapely flanks. Additionally, fine views west look to Ill Bell and High Street in eastern Lakeland.

Dropping gently down, a green, sunken way slants left, running on to eventually meet the beck. Here is the first of three fords that re-cross the stream, each accompanied by useful stones. If the crossing proves difficult, remain on the far bank to avoid two further crossings. Assuming the beck is not in spate, it has to be conceded that the track makes best use of the flats by its re-crossings. On returning to the far bank, the track runs faintly away from the beck to reach inflowing Great Nevy Beck alongside Nevygill Fold, an old sheepfold complex.

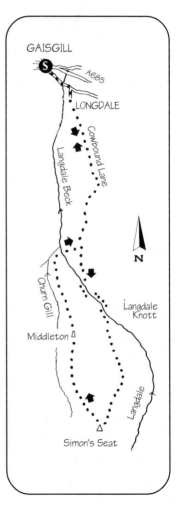

The fold is the one opportunity for real shelter out here, and its presence also confirms you're in the right place. **Cross this stream at the folds and leave at once by turning up the slope on the left, faint traces of quad tracks leading up the steep nab. The gradient soon relents and easier ground runs on to the head of Little Nevy Gill.** My March visit saw this draped in not insignificant cornices!

A full Lakeland skyline is arrayed over to the right now, with Great Gable upstanding as distinctly as ever. **Remain on the broad ridge top, rising to a second knoll and crossing minor peaty sections before finally gaining the rounded summit of Simon's Seat at 1925ft/587m.** It is marked by the only stones in view, forming a very neat little cairn. The all-round view is truly outstanding, featuring an unbroken distant Lakeland skyline, the Westmorland limestone plateau, Eden Valley, North Pennines, and the bulk of the main plateau of the Howgills immediately south. Here the Calf displays an unfamiliar aspect, unspectacular but nevertheless impressive.

The summit of Middleton, looking to Yarlside

The return leg commences by doubling gently back to the right down a long, narrowing spur running out to Middleton: keen eyes

Packhorse bridge, Langdale

will discern the white painted Ordnance Survey column out on the end. Descent to the col is very brief, followed by a fine level march in further minor quad tracks, the little pull at the end being negligible. At 1594ft/486m, Middleton's OS column (10798) is, like Simon's Seat's summit cairn, a lone figure. **From here resume again, at once starting to descend the ridge end. This is a longer drop on a good, light track, winding down to near the intake wall ahead and Langdale Beck on the right.** Ahead, the enclosed pastures and woods of lower Langdale appear truly delightful. **At the foot of the ridge bear across to the beck to reach a tiny, stone arched footbridge.** This hidden gem is the most obvious halting place on the walk, a lovely spot.

Cross the bridge and head straight up the grassy slope ahead, on a steep little pull between bracken patches to regain the sunken way. Continue up to the brow and follow the wallside track back to Cowbound Lane, and thence back down to the start.

16
HAZELGILL KNOTT & BOWDERDALE

START *Bowderdale Foot*   *Grid ref. NY 678045*

DISTANCE *8¼ miles/13km*

ORDNANCE SURVEY MAPS
1:50,000
Landranger 91 - Appleby-in-Westmorland
Landranger 98 - Wensleydale & Upper Wharfedale
1:25,000
Explorer OL19 - Howgill Fells/Upper Eden Valley

ACCESS *Bowderdale is signposted off the A685 west of Newbiggin-on-Lune. Park on the roadside just before it drops down to the beck and the buildings.*

A supremely simple return walk - the deep confines of Bowderdale contrast with the wide panoramas of its enclosing ridge. The return ridgewalk is not highly recommended in mist.

S Bowderdale Foot shelters in glorious seclusion, though is now just a little nearer the A685 since it was cynically rebuilt on the line of the Tebay-Darlington railway. **Cross the bridge over Bowderdale Beck and up the hill past the houses, and before a cattle-grid on the brow leave the road by a wallside track on the left. This same track runs through two enclosures before climbing to a gate onto the open fell, at the very foot of the Hazelgill Knott-West Fell ridge.**

Running left with the wall, the way forks when the wall drops to the beck. You shall return to this point, but for now ignore the tractor track up the ridge and opt for the path slanting down to begin a long walk up Bowderdale. A profoundly claustrophobic atmosphere haunts this trek, channelled between archetypal Howgill ridges. Prominent throughout is shapely Yarlside across the valley.

Always keeping its distance above the beck, the path forges on through this seemingly endless dale: only about 2½ miles since the fork does the time come to turn up the steep flank for the ridge top. This crucial point occurs after crossing inflowing Hazel Gill (note the lone tree part way up) just yards beyond Bowderdale Beck's major confluence with a similarly proportioned beck opposite. On arrival at the foot of Hazel Gill, walkers with the bit firmly between their teeth might opt to remain on the path as it climbs from the valley to eventually gain the summit of the Calf. A tiny tarn passed is the key to the path that returns along the Hazelgill Knott ridge.

Leave the valley path for the grassy shoulder, a direct climb that is less of a pull than it might appear. The going is aided by the terrace-like nature of the grass. As steepness relents advance across the broad ridge to intercept a clear track along its crest in the vicinity of some marshy pools. Turning right for home, first leave the track for the brief pull to Hazelgill Knott. At 1896ft/578m its unmarked summit is little more than a hundred feet beneath the magic 2000ft, happily so as this helps keep the place a lot quieter.

A steeper drop regains the track, and a little knoll is passed before an extended high-level march takes in the undulations of West Fell. Attention can now be firmly aimed at enjoying wide-ranging views beyond the Howgills' neighbours to the Westmorland limestone plateau, the Eden Valley, the North Pennines and, farther to the west, the Lakeland Fells. **Eventual descent leads off the end down to meet the outward route at the wall-corner.**

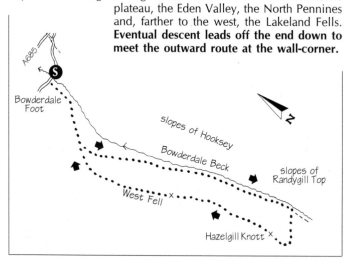

17

RANDYGILL TOP

START Weasdale   Grid ref. NY 693038

DISTANCE 6 miles/9½km

ORDNANCE SURVEY MAPS
1:50,000
Landranger 91 - Appleby-in-Westmorland
1:25,000
Explorer OL19 - Howgill Fells/Upper Eden Valley

ACCESS Start from the cul-de-sac road leading from the A685 at Newbiggin-on-Lune to Weasdale. Ample verge parking on the brow immediately before the road drops down into the hamlet. Newbiggin is served by infrequent Kirkby Stephen-Sedbergh bus.

The Weasdale Horseshoe: a straightforward circuit of a secret valley, visiting one of the Howgills' 2000-footers.

S **Descend the road to Weasdale Farm.** A branch right goes to Weasdale Nurseries, an enterprising venture at 850ft above sea level. **Go left past the farm, over the beck and up to an abrupt end at derelict Cow Bank.** On this brow Lakeland's eastern skyline appears, featuring Ill Bell and High Street. **A bridleway takes over, but your route is sharp left across the pasture to a crumbled barn and a wall. Advance with the wall to a gate in a fence onto the open fell of Hooksey.** Be sure to shut this, it is the only one on the walk!

Rise with the wall and a reedy old way to the wall corner. Now simply head up the grassy slope, trending left towards the Weasdale side of the broad ridge. Set back over to the left across Weasdale is Green Bell: the steep-sided valley is well seen, and this fell of your return route looms impressively large. Looking back, the patchwork fields of the upper Lune are backed by Cross Fell and its satellites.

Keeping left the going eases and a grassy old track should be met. Go left on this, running a largely contouring course along the fell's upper flank, very easy going as it rises imperceptibly and enjoys a full prospect over Weasdale and thus your horseshoe. Keeping below the ridge, this distinct green way runs for the best part of a mile before fading. Here turn up to the right to quickly gain a broader track on the ridge top. Resume on this, absorbing a further track as the final feet of ascent lead to the broad top of Hooksey.

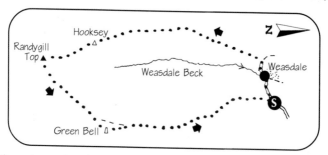

The cairn on Randygill Top briefly and misleadingly overtops your own imminent top, don't be fooled by it! To the right, behind, you have Yarlside, Great Dummacks at the top of Cautley Crag, Calders, the Calf and round to Fell Head. To the right of nearby Stockless are Wild Boar Fell and Swarth Fell. **The track fades just short of a tiny cairn at 1922ft/586m at the end of the plateau.**

Aiming south for Randygill Top, a faint path starts up and drops down to the intervening saddle of Leathgill Bridge. For a brief spell here there is nothing but high fells in view. Leathgill Bridge is a fine example of its kind, linking these two tops. **The climb up the other side is steep but quite short. As the going eases bear right, picking up a clear path rising gently to Randygill Top's summit cairn.** At 2051ft/625m this is the lowest of the five 2000ft mountains within the Howgills. Its sturdy cairn is a tribute to those who carted the stones here, presumably in recognition of a marvellous viewpoint.

The panorama includes, clockwise from the north, Cross Fell, Mickle Fell, Nine Standards Rigg, High Pike Hill, High Seat/Mallerstang Edge, Wild Boar Fell, Swarth Fell, Baugh Fell, Whernside above Rise Hill, Ingleborough, Great Coum, Middleton Fell, Yarlside and the fellow Howgills, and a long, uninterrupted Lakeland skyline.

Leave by heading north-east on a path declining gently towards the prominent Green Bell. This is the finest section of the walk, a high-level traverse on a sumptuous green path. A steady rise reaches a fork, as Green Bell's Ordnance Survey column re-appears just ahead. The original track, known as Scot Rake, swings left across the crest, having reached its highest point. Changing use has seen it usurped by the modern walkers' path that forges straight on up to Green Bell's waiting trig. point (10805) at 1985ft/605m.

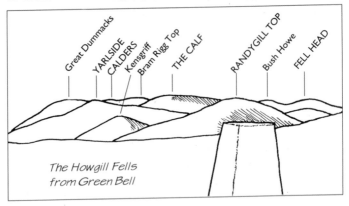

The Howgill Fells from Green Bell

It would be very difficult to find a better sub-2000ft viewpoint for England's varied mountain groups than this modest grassy felltop. Westwards is the serrated skyline of Lakeland; to the north the less dramatic but massive Cross Fell range; from east to south the summits of the Yorkshire Dales; while in front the Howgills appear as a well-defined mountain group, as illustrated.

Take the clear path striding north to begin an extremely rapid descent. Down the slope the old way eventually merges in from the left, keep straight on down. This fine tramp enjoys sweeping views over the upper Lune valley, beyond which are Sunbiggin Tarn reposing on the limestone plateau; Smardalegill Viaduct in its deep gorge; and beyond, the North Pennines (featuring High Cup's pronounced defile) above the receding Eden Valley. In time a walled pasture is reached on the left. On crossing another green track, keep left down the slope, nearing the wall and merging into a firmer track coming in from a wall on the left. Continue down this to soon join the wall and lead down to the start.

18

GREEN BELL

START *Ravenstonedale*   *Grid ref. NY 723042*

DISTANCE *6¾ miles/11km*

ORDNANCE SURVEY MAPS
1:50,000
Landranger 91 - Appleby-in-Westmorland
1:25,000
Explorer OL19 - Howgill Fells/Upper Eden Valley

ACCESS *Start from the village centre. Ample parking. Served by infrequent Sedbergh-Kirkby Stephen buses.*

Rolling hills, outstanding views, and near perfect solitude.

S Ravenstonedale is one of the loveliest old Westmorland villages, nestling at the foot of the Howgill Fells but also set below a limestone landscape spread to the north. A homely cluster of dwellings repose respectfully back from the attractive church. St Oswald's dates from the mid-18th century, and overlooks the site of a 12th century cell of Gilbertine canons. There are, surprisingly, two pubs and a pair of neighbouring chapels, one of 1839. Pleasant beck scenery, small greens, some charming cottages - look out for a surviving spinning gallery by the *Black Swan* - add to the delights of this village known locally as 'Rassendl'.

From the junction outside the school turn down to the bridge by the church, left to the *King's Head* and out on the road to the by-pass. Before the main road is reached, turn left up a 'no through road' to Greenside. Leave at the first gate on the right, following a wall away to enter an enclosed green lane. When it prematurely expires maintain the same line through the fields. These innocuous pastures mark the important Lune/Eden watershed, the major North-South

Cumbrian divide, with one river bound for Carlisle, the other for Lancaster. **Ultimately drop down past a barn and emerge via a drive onto a road-end at The Hollow.**

Go left with the road up towards a brow, but as a tractor track branches left, follow it onto the broad northern flanks of Green Bell. From gaining the open moor here, the route onto Green Bell's summit is already largely obvious. **Avoiding the moisture of Tailor Mire, the track makes a cautious start on the slope ahead. Occasionally sketchy, it slants ever half-right up past a fenced enclosure and soon improves as it rises to a well-defined corner above a walled enclosure. Rounding the bend it forks, and here take the upper branch curving onto the shoulder of Stwarth.**

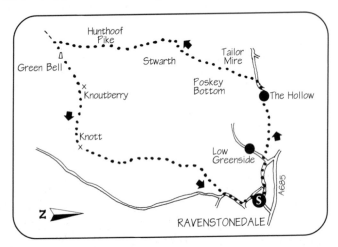

With the stones of Hunthoof Pike prominent ahead, a clear grass track climbs steadily up the better defined ridge. The 'pike' is found to require a detour. Hunthoof Pike has a flattering name, but is merely a tiny rash of stones from which a cairn has been fashioned. It does however, make a good viewpoint over deep-cut Great Swindale. In addition, the summit column now comes into view.

The track itself, meanwhile, rises ever more clearly to slant across Green Bell's upper cone to a saddle south-west of the top. This is a supreme moment, and now a clear path doubles back up to the

left to the waiting Ordnance Survey column (10805) at 1985ft/605m. Green Bell is, in the author's humble opinion, the finest sub-2000ft viewpoint for the varied mountain groups of England. Distantly is the serrated skyline of Lakeland, a joy to find in any picture; to the north is the less dramatic but nonetheless powerful Cross Fell range; from east to south are the individual summits of the Dales; while in front are the trusty Howgills, appearing in real style as a well-defined mountain group (illustrated on page 68).

The summit is vacated by a thin path heading east, almost at once dropping steeply to a sheepfold. The springs of Dale Gill below the fold are generally regarded as being the true source of the Lune. **Already in view is Ravenstonedale, and the finest way back utilises thin trods continuing east over the minor tops (both cairned) of Knoutberry and Knott. Striking north off the latter, a previously encountered path is joined above an island field.** Often sighted in this vicinity are grazing fell ponies, a regular feature of these foothills. **From the foot of this enclosure a super green track heads unerringly down the fell, emerging onto an access road to arrive at Town Head.**

An interesting finish avoids the road by crossing to a brace of wooden bridges on the left, thence dropping down through the 'back' of the village.

St Oswald's church, Ravenstonedale

71

19

STENNERSKEUGH & FELL END CLOUDS

START *The Street*   *Grid ref. NY 734005*

DISTANCE *3¾ miles/6km*

ORDNANCE SURVEY MAPS
1:50,000
Landranger 91 - Appleby-in-Westmorland
Landranger 98 - Wensleydale & Upper Wharfedale
1:25,000
Explorer OL19 - Howgill Fells/Upper Eden Valley

ACCESS *Start from an old quarry on the old road (The Street) just as it leaves the A683 Sedbergh-Kirkby Stephen road near Stennerskeugh (signposted Uldale and Fell End). Served by infrequent Sedbergh-Kirkby Stephen buses.*

An absorbing stroll through unfrequented limestone country that ranks with the finest.

S Stennerskeugh and Fell End Clouds present an extended limestone skirt on the lower flanks of Wild Boar Fell, which occupies the skyline. **From the quarry turn right (north) along the Street to join the main road, which is followed right for a minute only until the road shrugs off its attendant walls.**

Across the main road just before this corner is the location of an old Quaker burial ground, while even nearer the corner, on your side, is the site of a former toll bar. The Street is the name given to the old Sedbergh-Kirkby Stephen road, also enjoyed in WALK 24. It was superseded by the valley bottom road, which overlays it for only a short distance in the vicinity of the toll bar.

At the wall corner branch right with it on a grassy track. This runs along the front of Street Farm, and continuing on it becomes enclosed to pass between the buildings at the Street. Note the elaborate gateposts here. **Keep straight on (right) on the surfaced road to Stennerskeugh, and at the first opportunity double back up to the right on the walled track known as Clouds Lane.**

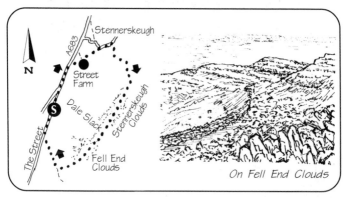

On Fell End Clouds

At a gate the track gains the open fell, **the most suitable right-hand track rising by the wall which soon swings right. Keeping above the wall, a pathless amble ensues along a grassy shelf sandwiched between tiers of limestone. These are Stennerskeugh Clouds, the highest point is about 1535ft/468m. Continue on until the pronounced hollow of Dale Slack, here turn up a green track taking advantage of the breach.** The panorama from the Clouds is magnificent, across the Westmorland plateau to the eastern Lakeland Fells and north to the North Pennines. Pride of place goes to the rounded tops of the nearby Howgill Fells, best appraised from Fell End Clouds.

Fell End Clouds are straight ahead now. When the track fades atop the outcrops turn right, again picking your own route influenced by the natural line of the scars. Fell End Clouds are particularly note-worthy for their composition of scars and pavements in crazy, irregular patterns. **Numerous cairns loiter about the pavements, and at the far end a single, substantial cairn precedes a lone tree by some old workings. These mark the terminus of the clouds, so bear down to the right well before Clouds Gill to pick up a thin track. This runs past two superbly preserved limekilns onto the Street. Turning right, its accommodating verge returns to the quarry.**

20

WANDALE HILL

START Cautley   Grid ref. SD 705975

DISTANCE 4½ miles/7km

ORDNANCE SURVEY MAPS
1:50,000
Landranger 98 - Wensleydale & Upper Wharfedale
1:25,000
Explorer OL19 - Howgill Fells/Upper Eden Valley

ACCESS Start from a lay-by on the A683, just south of Handley's Bridge (a long half mile north of the Cross Keys). Served by infrequent Sedbergh-Kirkby Stephen buses.

A simple ascent of an ordinary hill, but free of human life and enjoying outstanding mountain panoramas.

S **Go north along the road to Handley's Bridge, and turn left on the rough lane over the Rawthey. This is the drive to Northwaite, and swings left to rise into the farmyard.** Wandale Hill sends its long southern ridge down to the confluence of Westerdale and the Rawthey, and Northwaite occupies a fine position near the foot of this spur. **Cross the yard to a gate opposite, and follow the enclosed track rising right. At the top take the track alongside the left-hand wall, rising steadily as a green way to a gate onto the open hill.**

Over to the left is the bulk of Yarlside, with its ridge running north. **Continue rising on the green way, and when it levels out, double back up to the right on a similar old way, part-sunken as it slants up to meet the wall at an old sheepfold on the ridge. Turn left and turn up the broad grassy ridge, making a very steady, pathless ascent to the broad felltop. The tiniest of cairns can be found towards the back at 1630ft/497m, with a tiny pool nearby.**

The fell-dominated panorama features the Yarlside ridge to the west; Uldale straight across to the east, with Wild Boar, Swarth and Baugh Fells behind; the limestone scars of Stennerskeugh and Fell End Clouds of Wild Boar Fell under High Seat; and northwards the North Pennines. Note the well-defined line of farms and cottages on the Street, the old Sedbergh-Kirkby Stephen road under Wild Boar Fell.

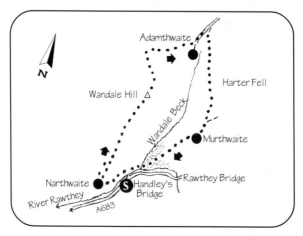

Resume north, dropping steadily down and heading for a large, walled enclosure opposite. A similar one on your side deflects you down to the left. In the bottom corner the walls, a tiny stream and the old green way that brought you out of Narthwaite meet. Pass through the gate and turn right along the field bottom. From a gate at the end a firm track heads away. At a fork the right branch drops steeply to Adamthwaite, but the left one maintains a steadier line to run on above a stand of larch and through bracken to drop down onto the farm road. Adamthwaite is the most isolated of Howgills farms, at the end of a near-three mile cul-de-sac from Ravenstonedale.

Go left and within 50 yards take a track on the right down to ford the beck. It climbs the other side by a wall then slants up to join a similarly splendid green way: turn right. Marching along the flank of Harter Fell, you can savour grand views over the enviably sited farmstead to Wandale Hill with the Yarlside ridge high behind. As the higher fells are lost behind Wandale Hill, the increasingly wooded side valley of Wandale Beck starts to dominate the scene.

A wall is joined and briefly followed before the now firmer track bears left over Murthwaite Rigg and merges into a farm road. Bear right along this to enter the extensive yard environs of Murthwaite. Don't drop down to the farmhouse but turn right on a track leading to a gate. Turn down the wallside (past a barn) to descend a large reedy pasture. When the fence on the left swings away, continue straight down the centre (the main road ahead is a guide) to enter the trees of Murthwaite Park. In this magnificent woodland I have been fortunate to observe deer and a red squirrel.

Looking over Adamthwaite to Wandale Hill, with Yarlside and Kensgriff behind

The aim is to arrive at the very foot of the broad ridge, preferably by finding a path that forms, slightly to the right. Succesfully located, it leads unerringly down to the bottom alongside Wandale Beck. Coming in from the right this ushers the path down to the corner of the wood, where you must ford the stream. There are reasonable stones unless in spate: in any case, you're only five minutes from the end, and dry footwear!

From a gate behind the beck, leave the woods on a grassy field track to a gate back onto Narthwaite farm road. Handley's Bridge is now just down to the left.

21

ULDALE WATERFALLS

START Rawthey Bridge   Grid ref. SD 711978

DISTANCE 5¾ miles/9km

ORDNANCE SURVEY MAPS
1:50,000
Landranger 98 - Wensleydale & Upper Wharfedale
1:25,000
Explorer OL19 - Howgill Fells/Upper Eden Valley

ACCESS Rawthey Bridge is astride the A683, on the National Park boundary 5½ miles from Sedbergh. There is a large parking area on the roadside just south of the bridge. Served by infrequent Sedbergh-Kirkby Stephen buses.

The sparkling Rawthey is in its element as it races through the rarely frequented Uldale. Uldale is the name given to the upper reaches of the Rawthey.

S By the National Park boundary sign a gate sends a track off into an uninspiring marsh. It quickly escapes to climb a grooved route to the right, and at the brow fords a marshy beck. This old track is the original highway through the hills, linking Sedbergh and Kirkby Stephen. Constructed well above the valley floor, it now forms a green promenade with outstanding views to the eastern Howgills: immediately upstream of the present bridge is the site of the old road's bridge (WALK 24 runs a longer section of this). **Here leave the old road (which heads off parallel with but high above the present road) by a branch sharp left, bound for a level march into Uldale.**

Your own green track into Uldale is itself an old road: generally a classic route underfoot, it may be less so if trail riders have recently exercised their bikes. Noise and dirt are not able to ruin the views, however, in which the retrospective Cautley scene is pre-eminent. On penetrating Uldale the more subtle grandeur of Wild Boar and Swarth Fells takes over. **The track is clear throughout as it runs along to arrive above a footbridge below the inflowing Needlehouse Gill, a bridge to which you shall return after visiting the waterfalls.**

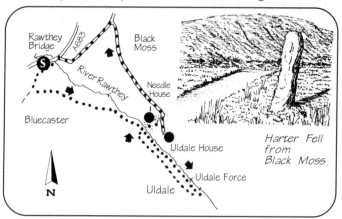

Harter Fell
from
Black Moss

Already the first falls are in view, and a thin path shadows the Rawthey to approach them and then climb past. Easy going on a sometimes sketchy path leads to a short, bouldery section below the wall of Rawthey Gill Quarry. Towards the end the splendid fall of Whin Stone Gill on the sidestream over to the left calls for a halt. Just beyond, a slight rise brings the walk's highlight, Uldale Force, into distant view. En route, however, a more modest waterfall intervenes, and this unexpected near-impasse necessitates a clamber up the steep slope, traversing cautiously above a sheer drop to permit further progress.

If satisfied with the view of Uldale Force from this point, then take advantage of height gained to rise again to locate a slim trod above the ravine. **For the full itinerary drop back towards the beck to forge on the final 200 yards - again with care near the end - to stand in the profound amphitheatre at the very foot of the tumbling waters.** Uldale Force is a major drop, Hardraw-like in its setting, but if anything a better fall of water. Here one pays in effort, rather than shillings, for the pleasure. Just above, and worth a visit, is a contrastingly delicate, open-air fall.

At Uldale Force, the path most emphatically terminates. Onward progress thus barred, retrace steps a few yards to scamper up the grassy bank to low outcrops lining the top. A slender trod is gained and facilitates an excellent return walk high along the edge of the gill's confines, offering a thorough overview which includes fresh sightings of Whin Stone Gill Falls and retrospects of Uldale Force. Little more than a sheeptrod, your way runs along to a fold, appropriately enough, then quickly peters out. By now it is about time to work a way steadily down to return to the footbridge.

Crossing the bridge, an enclosed track mounts the opposite flank, rising through woodland to meet the road to Uldale House. Turn left along it to merge with one from Needle House, thence running out across the moors of White Green and Black Moss. Passing a standing stone, look north to locate the gleam of limestone on Fell End Clouds (see WALK 19). The road leads out to a T-junction at Foggy Gill, part of the scattered hamlet of Fell End. Turn left along the equally quiet old road to drop tidily down to Rawthey Bridge.

Uldale Force

22

YARLSIDE

START *Cautley*   *Grid ref. SD 698969*

DISTANCE *5½ miles/9km*

ORDNANCE SURVEY MAPS
1:50,000
Landranger 98 - Wensleydale & Upper Wharfedale
1:25,000
Explorer OL19 - Howgill Fells/Upper Eden Valley

ACCESS *Start from the Cross Keys Inn on the A683. There is a lay-by just past it. Served by infrequent Sedbergh-Kirkby Stephen buses.*

A steep climb, a splendid short ridge, and leisurely walking to finish. Outstanding views include a lesser seen aspect of Cautley Spout.

S Boasting one of the finest settings imaginable, the *Cross Keys* is that rare creature the temperance inn. It is in the hands of the National Trust, and its legacy ensures that it is never likely to offer a pint of ale. The door lintel bears a 1732 datestone. Though labelled Cautley there is no definable centre, just a scattering of farms, dwellings and a church along the Sedbergh road.

From the Cross Keys cross the footbridge over the Rawthey beneath the lay-by. Note that an alternative route sets a direct course up the slope in front: the ascent is beautifully uncomplicated - just head uphill! The way is entirely grassy and not as steep as might appear as the opening slopes of Ben End are faced, before a saddle precedes the haul to meet the main route on the south top.

The main path turns left to head for Cautley Spout, so follow it around the base of Yarlside to enter this magnificent amphitheatre beneath Cautley Crag and Spout. The path advances invitingly to

the base of the ravine. Here, alongside a tiny sidestream, the ways fork. Leaving the rough branch left for WALK 23, take the contrastingly genteel right branch. Without the rigours of the other path, this affords a classic prospect of the tumbling falls of the Spout.

The path slants up above the sidestream as a delectable green way, zigzagging part way up to arrive on the saddle of Bowderdale Head. Beyond, the long valley of Bowderdale runs northwards to the upper Lune Valley. The second half of your ascent turns right to scale the steep grassy slopes onto Yarlside's rounded south top. Turn left to join a green trod for a short pull onto Yarlside's summit.

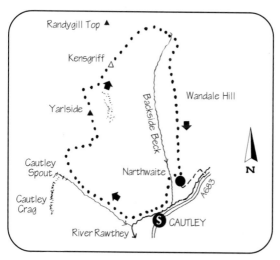

Marked by a lonely cairn at 2096ft/639m, this otherwise bare top is nevertheless a fine airy vantage. Look back to the upper section of Cautley Spout, with Great Dummacks, Calders, Bram Rigg Top and the Calf behind, and the western Howgills ridges arrayed. Eastwards are the Howgills' neighbours Wild Boar, Swarth and Baugh Fells.

Resume north-west along the ridge, avoiding thoughts of a bee-line for Kensgriff. You are now surrounded by a real Howgills atmosphere, with ridges and tops outspread, and looking directly down Bowderdale. Shapely Kensgriff, next along the ridge, is currently dwarfed by your present fell, but not so in 10 minutes time when looking up to it! **A trod from the cairn peters out on the steep northerly edge, and steep grassy slopes angle you down to the col, with Kensgriff now looking a fine little cone. A thin path runs up its ridge to quickly gain the cairn at 1883ft/574m.** Looking back, it will be seen why the direct approach was not recommended, Yarlside's scree slope being far too rough for comfort. Another small cairn sits lost on the summit.

On the ascent of Kensgriff, looking to Hazelgill Knott and a distant Lakeland skyline

Resume north again, once more with a modest path descending the easy-angled ridge to a saddle containing a pool beneath Randygill Top's dull slope. Ahead, Green Bell (see WALKS 17 and 18) is also prominent. Those wanting to 'bag' a second 2000-footer for the day can shoot up the slope on the left to quickly gain Randygill Top's cairn, though as WALK 17 makes it the pinnacle of another outing, I'll wait for you by the pool.

Passing the pool a little sidestream forms the upper limits of Stockless Gill. Descending on its right side an old, part-sunken path can be found to lead down above it for a while. When it fades simply forge on down the slope, well above the stream until aiming for a distinct confluence with Spen Gill beneath a rocky ravine ahead. The confluence is a fine spot to linger awhile and savour the charms. A couple of tasty waterfalls tumble through the rocky surrounds, and a natural rock garden is in evidence.

From the confluence either climb directly to reach a reedy track, or first go left up the bank to see more of the ravine before crossing reedy ground to find the initially faint old road on Wandale Hill's flank. Either way, turn right along this old way, soon leaving the marshy section behind for a contrastingly splendid green march. To the right your two shapely hills are admirably displayed.

Simply remain on this track, becoming firmer as it joins a wall and runs above the old farmhouse of Mountain View. This old farmstead boasts one of the finest locations in the district, though sadly it no longer accommodates daily life. The way continues, green again (with a spell as a narrower path above the actual reedy wallside way of the old road) and still delectable as it slants down to a gate. In similar fashion it runs down the wallside to become an old sunken lane just above the farm of Narthwaite.

Kensgriff, looking back to Yarlside

Entering the yard, take a gate down to the right into a grassy enclosure. A path winds down to the bottom right corner, where an enclosed way runs down past a fine array of hollies to a ford on Backside Beck. Ahead, Kensgriff bows out in shapely profile. There are ample stones to cross, but in spate wet feet are easily acquired: perhaps fortunately, the end is only minutes away. Take the path left up outside the trees, running delightfully on through open country, back on Yarlside's base to return to the Rawthey footbridge.

23

CAUTLEY CRAG & SPOUT

START Cautley   Grid ref. SD 698969

DISTANCE 5½ miles/9km

ORDNANCE SURVEY MAPS
1:50,000
Landranger 98 - Wensleydale & Upper Wharfedale
1:25,000
Explorer OL19 - Howgill Fells/Upper Eden Valley

ACCESS Start from the Cross Keys Inn on the A683. There is a lay-by just past it. An alternative start is Rawthey Bridge. Cautley is served by infrequent Sedbergh-Kirkby Stephen buses.

A justifiably famous corner of the Howgills, the splendour of Cautley Spout leading to an airy felltop and a grand descent and valley path.

Whilst every effort is made to ensure walks are described in the most enjoyable direction, many are just as good either way round. On this occasion, however, do not go clockwise! Whilst others may suggest descent by Cautley Spout, I wouldn't dream of recommending it to anyone out for a pleasurable walk.

S Cautley Crag and Spout combine to form the grandest scene in the Howgill Fells. The steep crag extends for the best part of a mile to an abrupt end at the Spout, which is a series of waterfalls tumbling in rapid succession for several hundred feet to the valley floor. Boasting one of the finest settings imaginable, the *Cross Keys* is that rare creature the temperance inn. It is in the hands of the National Trust, and its legacy ensures that it is never likely to offer a pint of ale. The door lintel bears a 1732 datestone. Though labelled Cautley there is no definable centre, just scattered farms, dwellings, St Mark's church and a Methodist Chapel of 1845 on the Sedbergh road.

Cross the footbridge over the Rawthey just above the inn, and go straight ahead onto a wide track. Turn left along it, quickly swinging in to the prized amphitheatre beneath Cautley Crag. The path is infallibly drawn towards the base of the falls, though more on the base of the fell than on the streamside. At the foot of the ravine the path forks. A gentle one climbs right, for Bowderdale Head, while the left branch crosses the tiny sidestream to tackle the path by the gill. The path is both rough and steep: extra caution is urged when peering into the lower fall, which is partially obscured by hardy foliage. Pausing to look back, Wild Boar, Swarth and Baugh Fells form a sombre mountain skyline.

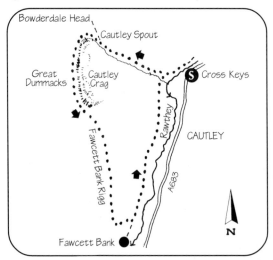

Continuing, the upper falls are free of obstruction and can be savoured more leisurely. After a steeper pull the path suddenly levels out. The main path bears left and runs splendidly on to cross the sidestream of Swere Gill, then rises round to meet the main stream, Red Gill Beck. Though the main path continues upstream, cross here and up a faint trod onto the spur of Great Dummacks above Cautley Crag.

This same path broadens and leads increasingly gently up the broadening spur above Cautley Crag, all the way to the highest point. The upper stages run along the grassy crest of the crags to

reveal some dramatic situations. The most sensational moment is saved for the far end, where a stony gully is the place to break journey. The gully provides a suitable foreground to the crag as it shrinks away towards the Spout: Yarlside forms an impressive wall behind, with lonely Bowderdale running away beyond the dip of Bowderdale Head. The tame slopes of the Calf rise to the Howgills' plateau.

Immediately above you, though in truth merely an aside, is the summit of Great Dummacks. Few walkers are likely to go seeking the errant high point of this broad plateau. At 2175ft/663m this is the least notable of the 2000ft tops of the Howgills; or at least it would be, if it wasn't for Cautley Crag....

Head south on the broad ridge of Fawcett Bank Rigg (aiming for distant Ingleborough, if the day be clear), a super amble after the excitement of Cautley Spout. Glorious views look out over several miles of the Rawthey's course to a mountain panorama, with Wild Boar Fell, Swarth Fell and Baugh Fell opposite, and the Dales peaks dominated by the celebrated Three Peaks of Penyghent, Whernside and Ingleborough.

Simply stride down this gentle ridge, an intermittent track on offer, until approaching a wall corner near the base of the ridge. Here (after crossing an intriguing ditch) deflect left with the wall, and at the next corner drop down by it to gain a track. This is the Sedbergh-Cautley bridleway. Turn left and it will lead unfailingly back. The Rawthey Valley makes fine company from your terrace well above the river. Besides the fells opposite, you have the easternmost Howgills pairing of Wandale Hill and Harter Fell ahead. **St Mark's church stands on the roadside below.**

After a spell beneath the gorse (then bracken) base of the fell, the narrowing path takes a small gate into a rough pasture. Beyond a second gate the path is fainter until resurrected at the stream ahead. On again, and beyond a gateway in an old wall, look out for a gate on the left to return through the intake wall to the base of the fell. Resume as before, soon reaching Cautley Holme Beck. Though it can usually be forded, a small footbridge upstream leads back into the basin of Cautley Crag: directly ahead are Yarlside's unremitting flanks. Bear right, tracing the Rawthey upstream to rejoin the outward route just short of the start.

Cautley Crag, with Bowderdale and the North Pennines beyond

24

CAUTLEY SPOUT & UPPER RAWTHEY

START Cautley   Grid ref. SD 698969

DISTANCE 6 miles/9½ miles

ORDNANCE SURVEY MAPS
1:50,000
Landranger 98 - Wensleydale & Upper Wharfedale
1:25,000
Explorer OL19 - Howgill Fells/Upper Eden Valley

ACCESS Start from the Cross Keys Inn on the A683. There is a lay-by just yards past it. An alternative start is Rawthey Bridge, a mile further north. Served by infrequent Sedbergh-Kirkby Stephen buses.

A splendid ramble around the higher reaches of the Rawthey, with glorious Howgills views and the grandeur of Cautley Spout to finish.

S Dated 1732, the *Cross Keys* is a rare example of a temperance inn. Cautley itself has no definable centre, just a scattering of farms, dwellings and a church (St Mark's) and Methodist Chapel of 1845 along the Sedbergh road.

Cross the footbridge over the Rawthey just above the inn, and go straight ahead onto a wide track. Turn right along it, continuing as a pleasant green path to ford Backside Beck (a challenge after a wet spell) before a short pull to Narthwaite. Leave the farm buildings by the drive on the right, following it almost all the way down to the main road. A gate on a sharp bend, however, points the way along a lesser track which ends at a wood. Through a gate, ford a stream to follow a path on the wood bottom, and when the fence turns right it slants down to follow the Rawthey upstream.

The river Rawthey flows for sixteen miles from near the lonely summit of Baugh Fell to its acceptance into the Lune beyond Sedbergh. On the journey there it absorbs the waters of the Clough and the Dee. All is preciously unspoilt hereabouts, and in the neighbourhood of this walk the river exudes all its charms, flowing along a green valley bottom with bare fells rising on each side.

Emerging from the trees to cross a brace of fields, a tiny stream is crossed (by a bridge, at last!) to rise onto the road just above Rawthey Bridge. Rawthey Bridge marks the historic Yorkshire-Westmorland boundary and, as a result, the illogical National Park boundary also. Between the unfortunately titled Backside Beck and the bridge you therefore tread a mile of old Westmorland.

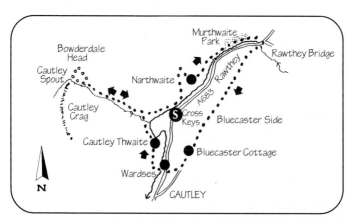

Within a few yards of crossing the bridge take a gate on the left, from where a track heading away almost at once turns sketchily right in a distinctly moist neighbourhood. The track soon improves, and after a gentle rise starts to run parallel with but high above the main road. On this section from Rawthey Bridge to beyond Bluecaster you tread the old road to Kirkby Stephen, formerly the main highway through these hills. Constructed well above the valley floor, it now forms a green promenade with truly outstanding views across to the eastern Howgills: the great bowl of Cautley is at the heart of this scene. Semi-wild ponies graze this open fell. **Shortly after passing Bluecaster Cottage a gate is reached at a lanehead, and just after it take a gate on the right to descend a sunken track onto the road.**

Cross the main road and down a farm road past Wardses. The farm bridge over the Rawthey here is surprisingly high: note the intense clarity of the water. **The track continues through the fields to Cautley Thwaite Farm. Keep straight on through two gates and to the right of a barn, then going a little left to a gate to emerge on a good path. Soon Cautley Holme Beck is crossed by a footbridge. For a direct finish advance straight on with the Rawthey.**

To enjoy a closer look at Cautley Spout, bear left to join the main path from the *Cross Keys*, which runs along to the foot of the ravine. Cautley Spout is a series of waterfalls which tumble in rapid succession for several hundred feet to the valley floor. An optional ascent by the falls earns intimate views: cross the tiny sidestream to the path by the gill. The path is both rough and steep: extra caution is urged when peering into the lower fall, which is partially obscured by hardy foliage.

Further up, the upper falls are free of obstruction and can be savoured more leisurely. After the steepest section the path levels out, and here leave it along a trod to the right. After a steady traverse slant down to the incisive pass of Bowderdale Head. Turning right a good path descends with the sidestream to the foot of the Spout. Return on the main path around the base of Yarlside, turning upstream with the Rawthey to quickly return to the footbridge at the start.

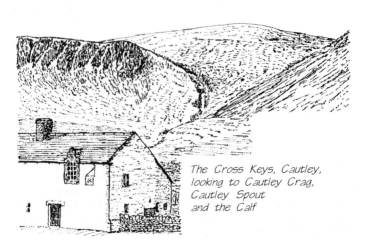

The Cross Keys, Cautley, looking to Cautley Crag, Cautley Spout and the Calf

LOWER GARSDALE

START *Garsdale Foot*   *Grid ref. SD 694912*

DISTANCE *6¼ miles/10km*

ORDNANCE SURVEY MAPS
1:50,000
Landranger 98 - Wensleydale & Upper Wharfedale
1:25,000
Explorer OL2 - Yorkshire Dales South/West (tiny section)
Explorer OL19 - Howgill Fells/Upper Eden Valley

ACCESS *Start from the large parking area on Longstone Common, some 2½ miles out of Sedbergh where the A684 Hawes road becomes unfenced.*

A modest stroll through fields and by fine riverbank in the shadow of giant fells. The walk concludes with a stroll along the Sedgwick Geological Trail: an informative leaflet can be obtained in Sedbergh.

S Garsdale is today probably the least known of any valley in the National Park - certainly for its size - though Norse settlers knew it well enough. Generally featureless hills rise steeply on either side, without a single right of way up either for many a long mile. The 'centre' of the dale is a very modest community called the Street some way up the valley. Most folks' only experience of Garsdale is through a car window en route from Sedbergh to Hawes.

Leave the car park by the minor road dropping down to cross the river Clough at Danny Bridge, to which you shall later return. Follow this traffic-free byway up-dale for a good mile and a half. Several farms are passed along the way. Eventually, after a short, steep pull just beyond a farm on a sharp bend, take a gate on the left labelled Bellow Hill. Follow the drive to the first wall, then branch right to a stile. Continue away with the wall to cross a

tiny beck, and on again to a stile before aiming for the farm of Pike Hill ahead. A stile gives access to its lane which can be followed down to the road.

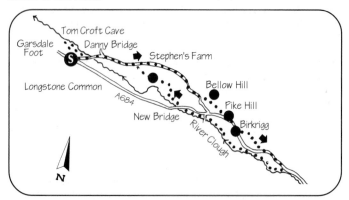

Go left for a quarter-mile or so. Greater care is needed here as this is the main road, not the back one, and its verges offer little refuge. At the allotted distance - just beyond the first farm on the right - locate a half-hidden stile on the left at a bend. Follow the wall away, crossing a drive and on through a second field to find the next stile just left of a barn. From a tiny beck rise over the field to a gate, then across to a stile back onto the road. Head left once again, the road thankfully being far more accommodating this time. As it swings down to the river, take up the offer of a stile just beyond a barn.

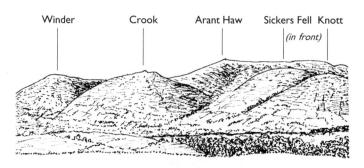

The Howgill Fells from Longstone Common

The return leg begins in the company of the Clough. At the end of the first pasture some trees briefly keep the river at bay, but otherwise a long and pleasant walk clings to the wooded bank all the way to New Bridge. While the main road crosses the river, the walk merely crosses the road to descend steps in order to resume downstream.

At the first field boundary however, it is time to leave the Clough and head up the fieldside towards a barn. Go through a hand-gate just before it, and up the small enclosure to a gate left of the barn. Slant half-left up to a stile, then head along through several fields to arrive at the front of Stephen's Farm. Continue across until Hole House Farm appears, and from a gate at the right side of a tiny plantation its yard will be entered.

The farm drive heads away to rejoin the outward lane, to return to Danny Bridge. On crossing it, a flourishing finish incorporates the Sedgwick Geological Trail. This well-designed trail is named after renowned geologist Professor Adam Sedgwick, born in neighbouring Dentdale in 1785 and spending 50 years at Cambridge. In recognition of his research locally, a detailed leaflet tells what to look for in this remarkable area of the important Dent Fault. The trail simply follows the river Clough downstream from Danny Bridge for a short distance on a permissive path. It ends beyond a short fenced section, and an initially sketchy path slants back up to the car park. Numerous features of note are seen, including Tom Croft Cave on the opposite bank, shortly before returning.

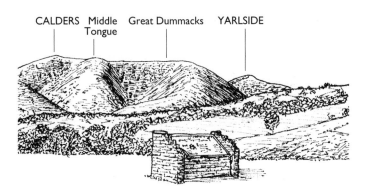

CALDERS Middle Great Dummacks YARLSIDE
         Tongue

SOME USEFUL ADDRESSES

Ramblers' Association
2nd Floor, Camelford House, 87-89 Albert Embankment, London SE1 7BR
Tel. 020-7339 8500

Yorkshire Dales National Park Information Services
Colvend, Hebden Road, Grassington, Skipton, N. Yorkshire BD23 5LB
Tel. 01756-752748

Tourist Information, 72 Main Street **Sedbergh** LA10 5AD
Tel. 01539-620125
Tourist Information, 22 Market Street **Kirkby Stephen** CA17 4QN
Tel. 017683-71199
Tourist Information, Town Hall, Highgate **Kendal** LA9 4DL
Tel. 01539-725758

Cumbria Tourist Board
Ashleigh, Holly Road, Windermere LA23 2AQ
Tel. 015394-44444

Yorkshire Dales Society
Otley Civic Centre, Cross Green, Otley, W. Yorkshire LS21 1HD
Tel. 01943-461938

Friends of the Lake District *(covers the whole of Cumbria)*
Murley Moss, Oxenholme Road, Kendal LA9 7SS
Tel. 01539-720788

East Cumbria Countryside Project
Warwick Mill, Warwick Bridge, Carlisle CA4 8RR
Tel. 01228-561601
(maintains rights of way in the Upper Eden section)

The Woodland Trust
Autumn Park, Dysart Road, Grantham, Lincolnshire NG31 6LL
Tel. 01476-581135

Public transport
Traveline 0870-608 2608

National Rail Enquiry Line 08457-484950

LOG OF THE WALKS

WALK	DATE	NOTES
1		
2		
3		
4		
5		
6		
7		
8		
9		
10		
11		
12		
13		
14		
15		
16		
17		
18		
19		
20		
21		
22		
23		
24		
25		

INDEX

Principal features: walk number refers